Effective Co-Parenting or Parallel Parenting With A Narcissist

Set Boundaries, Eliminate Conflict, Protect Yourself, and Raise Emotionally Secure Children

Claire Brown

Contents

Foreword

We recognize, honor, and respect that families are formed in various ways, and not every parent is involved in a marriage and divorce. For this book and purposes of simplicity, we use the term "divorce" to indicate that children are raised by parents living in separate homes and the term "ex" to refer to your ex, the other parent of your children.

Introduction

The moment of clarity came during yet another heated exchange, not unlike countless others before it. But this time, amidst the frustration and despair, there was a profound realization: the traditional advice and strategies for co-parenting were inadequate to handle the unique challenges of dealing with a narcissistic ex. This epiphany wasn't just a personal turning point; it marked the beginning of a journey to find a better way—a way that always keeps the well-being of the children at the forefront. In recent years, the complexities of co-parenting or parallel parenting with a narcissistic ex-partner have become an increasingly urgent concern for many parents. The journey is fraught with emotional and practical challenges, intensified by the unique dynamics of dealing with a narcissist. Despite the growing need for guidance, there remains a stark lack of comprehensive resources dedicated to addressing both the emotional turmoil and the practical steps necessary for minimizing conflict and fostering a nurturing environment for children. This book aims to fill that gap, offering a lifeline to those who feel overwhelmed and under-supported.

The core thesis of this book is that successful co-parenting or parallel parenting with a narcissistic ex is not only possible but can be a pathway to personal growth and healthier family dynamics. It hinges on a deep understanding of narcissistic behaviors, the strategic implementation of boundaries, and the selection of the most appropriate parenting style tailored to individual circumstances.

My journey into the realm of co-parenting with my narcissistic ex was neither straightforward nor easy. I remember the initial confusion, the fear, the worry, the constant second-guessing, and the overwhelming sense of isolation. It was a period marked by trial and error, with each step forward seemingly matched by at least two steps back. However, through persistent effort and a commitment to understanding the underlying dynamics at play, I discovered effective strategies for managing the relationship with my ex-partner and ensuring the well-being of our children. It is this journey, from dysfunction to clarity, that I wish to share with you, offering not just advice but a reflection of shared experiences.

This book is structured to guide you through the intricacies of raising children with a narcissist, explaining co-parenting and parallel parenting options, and detailing practical strategies for conflict resolution. It delves into the legal and emotional support structures that can aid this process, offering actionable advice and expert insights. What sets this book apart is its comprehensive approach, addressing not just the theoretical underpinnings of narcissism but also providing a hands-on guide to navigating the day-to-day challenges it presents in co-parenting scenarios.

To the dedicated parents who have picked up this book, seeking to shield their children from the fallout of a relationship with a narcissistic ex and to find a path forward for their healing, this book is for you. It acknowledges the difficulties you face and affirms that with the proper knowledge, tools, and confidence, navigating co-parenting with a narcissistic ex can lead to a healthier, happier family dynamic.

Let this book be your resource. Use it to engage deeply with its content, apply the strategies it outlines, and join a community of individuals who share your challenges and aspirations. You can move beyond the constraints of your past relationships to create a nurturing, positive environment for your children.

Thank you for placing your trust in this book. Your courage in seeking solutions and commitment to improving your family's life is commendable. With the help of this book, you will learn the necessary techniques and strategies to raise mentally healthy and happy children and move forward with your own lives with renewed strength and optimism.

Chapter 1
Understanding The Narcissist

Raising children is hard; raising children with an ex with whom you have an amicable relationship is manageable; raising children with an ex with whom there is conflict is difficult, and raising children with a narcissist is another level. Raising children with a narcissistic ex demands an extra layer of insulation for both you and the children. Understanding the behaviors characteristic of narcissism and their impact on co-parenting dynamics is critical; it's indispensable for maintaining your course and safeguarding your children's emotional health.

IDENTIFYING NARCISSISTIC BEHAVIORS AND THEIR IMPACT ON CO-PARENTING

Narcissistic behaviors, characterized by a lack of empathy, a need for admiration, and a sense of entitlement, can significantly disrupt the cooperative and harmonious effort required in co-parenting. These behaviors often manifest in ways that directly affect the co-parenting dynamic, making it imperative to recognize and address them effectively.

At the core of narcissistic behaviors is the inability or unwillingness to recognize and validate the feelings and needs of others, including one's own children. This fundamental lack of empathy often leads to situations where the narcissistic parent prioritizes their desires over the well-being of their children, viewing them more as extensions of themselves rather than independent individuals with distinct needs.

For example, consider deciding on extracurricular activities for the children. A narcissistic ex-partner might insist on selecting activities that either reflect well on them or that they enjoy, disregarding the children's interests or the practicality of the schedule for the primary caregiver. This can lead to conflicts that are not just about the activities themselves but underscore a deeper issue: the narcissistic parent's inability to consider and prioritize the children's preferences and the logistical needs of the family unit.

The need for admiration and validation, another hallmark of narcissistic behavior, often translates into a co-parenting context as a constant competition for the children's affection and loyalty. This can manifest in various ways, from extravagant gifts during visitations to disparaging remarks about the other parent, all aimed at securing the children's favor. Such actions strain the co-parenting relationship and place the children in an uncomfortable and unfair position where they feel torn between their parents.

Moreover, the sense of entitlement inherent in narcissistic behaviors can lead to unreasonable demands and expectations in the co-parenting arrangement. This might include expecting flexibility from the other parent without being willing to reciprocate or insisting on making unilateral decisions about the children's lives. These behaviors not only create a toxic atmosphere for co-parenting but also model unhealthy relationship dynamics for the children.

Addressing the impact of narcissistic behaviors on co-parenting requires a multifaceted approach. It involves setting clear and firm boundaries, both for the interactions with the narcissistic ex-partner and in terms of what behaviors the children are exposed to. It also necessitates maintaining open lines of communication with the children, providing them with a stable and reassuring presence amidst the unpredictable behaviors of the narcissistic parent.

Critically, it is essential to foster an environment where the children feel safe expressing their feelings and thoughts about the co-parenting situation. This could involve regular check-ins where the children are encouraged to share their experiences and concerns, ensuring they know their perspectives are valued and considered in decision-making processes.

Furthermore, seeking support from professionals, such as therapists or counselors, can provide not just emotional support for navigating co-parenting with a narcissistic ex-partner but also practical strategies for managing interactions and protecting the children's well-being.

In essence, recognizing and addressing the impact of narcissistic behaviors on co-parenting is not about engaging in a battle with the narcissistic ex-partner. Rather, it's about prioritizing the emotional health and stability of the children, ensuring they have the support and resources they need to thrive despite the challenges. This requires resolve, patience, resilience, and, above all else, a steadfast commitment to the well-being of the children.

THE SPECTRUM OF NARCISSISM: FROM TRAITS TO DISORDER

Narcissism, often misunderstood, stretches across a broad spectrum, revealing itself through a range of behaviors from subtle self-centeredness to the more severe Narcissistic Personality Disorder (NPD). Gaining insight into this spectrum is pivotal for parents striving to navigate the turbulent waters of co-parenting with a narcissistic ex. Recognizing where on this continuum the behavior of an ex-partner falls can significantly influence the strategies employed for managing interactions and safeguarding the emotional well-being of children involved.

At one end of the spectrum, we find individuals who exhibit narcissistic traits. These traits may include an inflated sense of self-importance, a deep need for excessive attention and admiration, and a lack of empathy for others. However, these traits do not entirely dominate the individual's personality or interactions. In co-parenting scenarios, this might manifest as occasional demands for undue attention or uncooperative behavior, yet these instances are sporadic and may not severely disrupt parenting dynamics.

Moving along the spectrum, the intensity and frequency of these traits increase, and so does their impact on co-parenting. The middle of the spectrum is where we often see a significant struggle for control and a pervasive pattern of manipulative behaviors aimed at undermining the other parent's authority or relationship with the children. This is a critical point where the behaviors start to resemble those associated with Narcissistic Personality Disorder, though they may not yet meet the clinical threshold for diagnosis.

The far end of the spectrum is where narcissistic traits condense into a full-blown dis-order. NPD is characterized by a persistent pattern of grandiosity, a constant need for admiration, and a lack of empathy, significantly affecting all areas of an individual's life, including co-parenting. Parents with NPD may view their children as mere extensions of themselves, disregarding the children's needs and feelings unless they align with their own. This can lead to a highly toxic co-parenting environment, fraught with conflict, manipulation, and emotional distress for both the children and the co-parent.

Understanding the spectrum of narcissism aids in tailoring co-parenting strategies to the specific challenges posed by an ex-partner's behaviors. For instance, dealing with someone who exhibits mild narcissistic traits might involve setting firm yet fair boundaries and engaging in mediated communication to minimize conflict. On the other hand, co-par-enting with an individual who has NPD may require more stringent boundaries, reliance on legal agreements to enforce co-parenting arrangements, and possibly limiting direct contact to protect the emotional and psychological well-being of the children.

It's also crucial for the co-parent to recognize the fluidity of the narcissism spectrum. Stress, life changes, and other factors can cause shifts in behavior, necessitating adjust-ments in co-parenting strategies. For example, an ex-partner exhibiting mild narcissistic traits may display more severe behaviors under stress, requiring a temporary increase in boundaries or support.

Understanding Narcissism's Impact on Children

Children are particularly susceptible to the effects of narcissistic behaviors, and the impact varies depending on where an ex-partner falls on the narcissism spectrum. Children exposed to mild narcissistic traits may experience moments of confusion or emotional distress when their needs are overlooked or when they witness conflicts between their parents. However, these effects can be mitigated with appropriate support and commu-nication from the non-narcissistic parent.

Conversely, children of a parent with NPD face more significant challenges. They may struggle with issues of self-esteem, develop an unhealthy understanding of relationship dynamics, or even mirror narcissistic behaviors. In these cases, it is paramount for the co-parent to provide a stable, empathetic environment where the children feel valued, heard, and respected. Open dialogues about emotions, reinforced boundaries, and professional support can help children navigate and understand their experiences without internalizing the negative aspects of their interactions with the narcissistic parent.

Strategies for Coping

For co-parents, developing effective strategies for managing interactions with a narcissistic ex-partner involves a blend of personal resilience, legal safeguards, and psychological support. This might include:

- Engaging in therapy or support groups to bolster emotional resilience and gain insights into effectively dealing with a narcissistic ex.

- Utilizing legal and formal arrangements to define clear co-parenting boundaries and responsibilities, thereby limiting the chance for manipulative behaviors.

- Adopting communication tools and strategies, such as parenting apps or third-party communication services, minimizes direct conflict and ensures that interactions remain focused on the children's well-being.

In essence, understanding the spectrum of narcissism enriches a parent's toolkit for navigating co-parenting with a narcissistic ex. It allows for a nuanced approach that protects the children's emotional health and supports the non-narcissistic parent's well-being, fostering a more stable and positive environment for everyone involved.

HOW NARCISSISM AFFECTS DECISION-MAKING IN PARENTING

In co-parenting with a narcissistic ex, the terrain is often marked by decision-making processes that sideline the needs and well-being of the children. These decisions can range in importance from daily routines to education choices and healthcare needs. This detour from child-centric decision-making is primarily due to the narcissist's characteristic traits, which skew their priorities and perceptions, often placing their desires and ego above all else.

The Ego at the Helm

One of the most evident ways narcissism affects decision-making in parenting is the prioritization of the narcissist's ego. For instance, in deciding on extracurricular activities, a narcissist might push for their children to enroll in prestigious or competitive programs—not for the children's enjoyment or growth but to bolster the parents' social standing or fulfill their unmet aspirations. This insistence often overlooks whether the child has an interest or aptitude in the activity, sometimes leading to stress, unhappiness, and a sense of inadequacy in the child.

Control as a Compass

The drive for control is another factor steering the narcissistic parent's decision-making. This need can manifest in micro-managing the children's schedules, interactions, and even thoughts, leaving little room for the children to express themselves or make choices about their lives. A controlling approach can stifle the children's independence and erode their confidence as they learn their desires and opinions hold little weight in the family dynamics.

The Mirage of Mutual Decisions

Co-parenting ideally involves collaboration and mutual decisions that benefit the children. However, with a narcissistic co-parent, this partnership often becomes a facade. The narcissistic parent might agree to joint decisions in theory but frequently undermines this agreement in practice, either by disregarding previously made decisions or by manipulating circumstances to ensure the outcomes align with their wishes. This inconsistency can confuse children and disrupt the stable environment they need, teaching them that agreements are not to be trusted and that authority figures may not act in their best interest.

The Reflection in the Mirror

Narcissistic parents often view their children as extensions of themselves rather than individuals with their own needs and rights. This perspective heavily influences their decision-making. Choices about the children's lives are made with an eye to how they reflect on the parent, leading to situations where children are pushed into roles or paths that echo the narcissist's self-image or aspirations. The children's actual talents, interests, and well-being become secondary if considered at all.

Strategies for Navigating Narcissistic Decision-Making in Parenting

Navigating this landscape requires strategies that prioritize the children's needs while managing the challenges posed by the narcissistic co-parent's decision-making style. Some approaches include:

- **Documenting Agreements**: Keeping a documented written record of all decisions and agreements can provide a reference point for discussions and help hold the narcissistic co-parent accountable for adhering to joint decisions. It is beneficial to timestamp all documents and arrangements.

Co-Parenting Apps: Thankfully, there are now several apps you can purchase and use to manage interaction with your ex. If you are dealing with a narcissistic ex-partner, this can be the solution to many of your problems. Utilizing these apps will allow you to drastically limit your contact with your ex, document and record exchanges, add a layer of transparency to all communication, and eliminate your ex's ability to manipulate events. Courts accept some of these apps, and they can be extremely helpful in family court rulings. These apps cost money, either a one-time fee or a subscription plan, and they are worth every penny. Below are some of the most robust apps on the market, with some of their main features highlighted. Do your own research and find the app that best fits your family dynamic and needs. If you are working with a family lawyer and/or a GAL, ask which app they recommend and which are accepted by the local court. Having a documented record that your local court accepts is a valuable resource.

Additionally, these apps can remove much of the conflict from engaging with a narcissist and will improve the quality of your life. They will document all of your communication, timestamp it, and are permanent. A narcissist will be unable to "spin" the information in these apps, and this will significantly diminish their power. Messages cannot be edited or deleted; this boxes the narcissist in and prevents wild claims and lying. It is a perfect tool for dealing with a narcissist and will also give you peace of mind. Many of these co-parenting apps also allow you to upload documents.

Our Family Wizard www.ourfamilywizard.com

Court-approved and recommended by many family law practices. Everything is time-stamped, and nothing can be deleted.

the main features include a shared calendar, video calls and traditional calls, messages, expenses, an important information vault, a journal for documenting anything that comes up, and a tone meter to keep all communications civil.

Talking Parents www.talkingparents.com

The main features include accountable calling, secure messaging, unalterable records, shared calendar accountable payments, an info library, a personal journal, and an attachment library.

2Houses www.2houses.com

The main features include a shared calendar, information vault, finance tracker, and journal.

Appclose www.appclose.com

The main features include a shared calendar, a secure message center where messages cannot be deleted, a request center, audio and video calls, and an expense center.

CoParenter www.coparenter.com

The main features include mediation, check-ins, a shared calendar, and records.

- **Guardian Ad Litem (GAL)** is an individual the court appoints, either upon request of one of the parents or when the court determines a GAL is necessary due to high conflict and constant issues. GALs are often lawyers and/or social workers who have taken courses and have extensive experience resolving parental disputes, putting the children's best interests first. Many family law practitioners recommend having a GAL when one parent is a narcissist. There is an added expense with enlisting the help of a GAL, but they can be an incredible resource for you and your children and remove conflict from your lives.

- **Empowering the Children**: Where appropriate, involving the children in decision-making processes can help counteract the effects of the narcissistic parent's control and ego-driven choices. This involvement should be age-appropriate and aim to empower the children, giving them a voice in matters that affect them.

- **Seeking Mediation and Legal Support**: In cases where the narcissistic parent's decision-making severely undermines the children's well-being or violates co-parenting agreements, seeking mediation or legal intervention can be necessary. Legal professionals and mediators familiar with narcissistic behaviors can offer strategies and interventions that protect the children's interests.

- **Fostering Open Communication**: Encouraging open communication within the family helps children understand they can express their needs and opinions. This communication should be a two-way street, where children feel heard and supported, contrasting the dynamics they might experience with the narcissistic parent.

- **Building a Support Network**: Surrounding the family with a supportive network of friends, relatives, and professionals can provide alternative perspectives and emotional support. This network can offer the children additional models of healthy relationships and decision-making.

In essence, while the narcissistic parent's decision-making processes in parenting present significant challenges, understanding these dynamics and employing targeted strategies can mitigate their impact. The goal is always to ensure that the children's needs and well-being remain at the forefront of all parenting decisions, fostering an environment where they can thrive despite the complexities of co-parenting with a narcissist.

EMOTIONAL MANIPULATION TACTICS USED BY NARCISSISTIC PARENTS

Narcissistic parents often resort to a range of emotional manipulation tactics that, without a doubt, introduce a layer of complexity to co-parenting. These tactics are not always overt; many operate under the guise of concern or affection, making them particularly insidious and challenging to counteract. Understanding these tactics is the first step in safeguarding both your and your children's emotional well-being.

Gaslighting: Undermining Reality

A prevalent form of manipulation used by narcissistic parents is gaslighting. This tactic involves questioning the validity of your experiences and memories, leading you to doubt your perceptions and sanity. In co-parenting, this might manifest as the narcissistic parent denying past agreements or conversations or insisting that events occurred differently than you remember, especially regarding decisions that affect the children. It's a disorienting experience that can leave you second-guessing yourself and, over time, erode your confidence in your parenting decisions.

Triangulation: Creating Divisions

Another tactic is triangulation, where the narcissist manipulates relationships between the people around them to maintain control and keep the focus on themselves. In a co-parenting scenario, the narcissistic parent might pit the children against you by sharing selective information or outright lies, creating an alliance with the children that excludes and isolates you. This not only strains your relationship with your children but also shifts the family dynamics in favor of the narcissist, making co-parenting even more challenging.

Love Bombing: The Cycle of Idealization and Devaluation

Love bombing is a tactic characterized by excessive affection, praise, and attention, followed by cold withdrawal or criticism. Narcissistic parents might shower their children with gifts and affection when they comply with their wishes but become distant or punitive when the children express needs or desires that diverge from the narcissist's agenda. This creates a confusing environment for the children, who learn that love and approval are conditional and dependent on meeting the narcissistic parent's often unreasonable expectations.

Projection: Shifting Blame

Projection involves the narcissist attributing their negative traits or behaviors to you, effectively shifting blame and avoiding accountability. For example, a narcissistic parent might accuse you of being selfish or uncaring when you enforce boundaries or make decisions aimed at protecting the children's best interests. This deflects from their shortcomings and attempts to paint you in a negative light, both in your eyes and those of your children, undermining your authority and relationship with them.

Silent Treatment: Control Through Withdrawal

The silent treatment is a form of emotional withholding used by narcissistic parents as a punishment or means of control. When displeased with a co-parenting decision or seeking to exert pressure, the narcissist may refuse to communicate, ignoring attempts at discussion or negotiation. This tactic can be particularly harmful, as it stalls productive co-parenting efforts and models unhealthy communication patterns for the children.

Playing the Victim: Manipulating Sympathy

Narcissistic parents often play the victim to elicit sympathy and manipulate situations to their advantage. By portraying themselves as the wronged party in co-parenting disputes, they seek to gain the children's and others' sympathy, casting you as the aggressor. This not only diverts attention from their problematic behaviors but also manipulates the narrative to undermine your credibility and relationship with the children.

Strategies for Counteracting Emotional Manipulation

Recognizing these tactics is crucial, as is developing strategies to counteract them effectively. Here are some approaches:

- **Document interactions**: Keeping a record of all communications can help you maintain a clear perspective and counteract gaslighting attempts. Consider getting a journal dedicated to documenting your interactions with your ex or an online, password-protected journal to document the interactions.

- **Strengthen your relationship with your children**: Open and honest communication can help mitigate the effects of triangulation and love bombing, ensuring your children feel valued and heard.

- **Set clear boundaries**: Establishing and enforcing boundaries with the narcissistic parent can protect you from tactics like the silent treatment and projection.

- **Seek professional support**: Engaging with a therapist or counselor can provide you with the tools to navigate the emotional challenges of co-parenting with a narcissist.

- **Educate yourself**: Understanding narcissism and its impact on family dynamics can empower you to respond more effectively to manipulation attempts.

- **Build a support network**: Surrounding yourself with understanding friends, family, and support groups can offer the emotional backing you need to navigate co-parenting challenges.

Facing a narcissistic co-parent requires resilience, patience, and a firm commitment to prioritizing the well-being of your children above the turmoil. By understanding and countering the emotional manipulation tactics employed by narcissistic parents, you can create a more stable and supportive environment for your children, ensuring they thrive despite the challenges.

UNDERSTANDING NARCISSISTIC SUPPLY AND ITS ROLE IN CO-PARENTING

In the intricate dance of co-parenting with a narcissistic ex, the concept of "narcissistic supply" emerges as a pivotal factor influencing their behavior and interactions. At its core, narcissistic supply refers to the sustenance derived from external sources that feed a narcissist's ego, affirming their sense of superiority and entitlement. This supply can come in various forms, including admiration, validation, attention, and even conflict, as long as it reinforces the narcissist's self-perception of importance and control.

Recognizing the role of narcissistic supply in co-parenting scenarios is crucial for anticipating potential challenges and strategizing effective responses. It sheds light on the motivations behind the narcissistic parent's actions, helping the co-parent understand that these behaviors often stem from a deep-seated need for validation rather than a genuine interest in the children's well-being or a desire to foster a collaborative co-parenting relationship.

The Quest for Supply through Children

Narcissistic parents might view their children as convenient sources of narcissistic supply, using their achievements, appearance, or behaviors as reflections of their own worth. This dynamic can manifest in various ways:

- **Exploiting Achievements**: A narcissistic parent may excessively tout their child's successes, treating them as personal accomplishments. This can place undue pressure on the children to perform or conform to their parent's expectations to avoid withdrawal of affection or approval.

- **Image Crafting**: Narcissists often curate the appearance of a perfect family to the outside world, using social media or public appearances to garner admiration. The children's needs or feelings may be secondary to maintaining this façade.

- **Emotional Feeding**: In more subtle forms, narcissistic parents might elicit emotional reactions from their children—be it positive attention or distress—as a means to feel powerful and indispensable.

Understanding these dynamics helps the co-parent protect their children from being used as pawns in the narcissist's quest for supply. It involves fostering an environment where children can pursue their interests and express their emotions freely, without fear of retribution or the burden of fulfilling the narcissistic parent's needs for validation.

Conflict as a Source of Supply

Surprisingly, conflict can also serve as a potent source of narcissistic supply. Engaging in disputes, especially those that evoke strong emotional reactions, can affirm the narcissist's sense of control and superiority. In co-parenting, this might translate into provoking arguments over parenting decisions or custody arrangements, often disregarding the impact such conflicts may have on the children.

To navigate this challenging aspect, it becomes vital to adopt strategies that minimize opportunities for conflict, such as:

- **Structured Communication**: Utilizing third-party communication services or adhering to written forms of communication can help maintain focus on parenting matters and reduce the potential for emotional provocation.

- **Boundary Setting**: Clearly defined boundaries, communicated calmly and consistently, can deter attempts to instigate conflict, as they limit the narcissist's ability to elicit an emotional response.

- **Legal Frameworks**: In cases where conflict escalates, turning to legal frameworks and custody agreements can provide a structured approach to resolving disputes, minimizing direct confrontation.

The Role of Admiration and Attention

For narcissists, admiration from others serves as a critical form of supply, affirming their grandiose self-image. In co-parenting, this might manifest in an overemphasis on public recognition or accolades related to parenting. The narcissistic parent may go to great lengths to be seen as the "ideal" parent, often at the expense of genuine, nurturing interactions with their children.

Similarly, the narcissist's need for attention can lead to behaviors that overshadow or undermine the co-parent's role and relationship with the children. This might include grand gestures or promises, unrealistic portrayals of lifestyle and opportunities, or monopolizing conversations and decisions about the children's lives.

To counteract these tendencies, it's essential to reinforce the value of authentic, supportive parenting behaviors over superficial displays of affection or commitment. To do this, you should:

- **Encouraging Real Connection**: Promoting activities and interactions that foster genuine connections between the narcissistic parent and the children can help shift the focus from external validation to the children's emotional needs.

- **Modeling Healthy Relationships**: Demonstrating healthy relationship dynamics, including respect, empathy, and cooperation, sets a positive example for the children and contrasts with the narcissist's often self-centered approach.

- **Supporting the Children's Perspectives**: Empowering children to express their needs and opinions regarding their relationship with the narcissistic parent encourages a more balanced and authentic family dynamic.

In essence, understanding the concept of narcissistic supply and its manifestations in co-parenting scenarios equips the co-parent with the insight needed to navigate the complexities of interacting with a narcissistic ex. It highlights the importance of strategies focused on minimizing conflict, fostering genuine connections, and prioritizing the children's emotional well-being above the narcissist's demands for attention and admiration. By recognizing the underlying motivations of the narcissistic parent's behaviors, co-parents can better protect their children from being used as sources of narcissistic supply and ensure a more stable, supportive environment for their growth and development.

Chapter 2

The Silent Echoes of Emotional Distress

C hildren can show stress and unhappiness when their needs are not being met. It is important to be on the lookout for any emotional turmoil they may be experiencing as a result of the narcissistic parent. As the stable parent, you can provide a solid foundation for them and counteract some of their unease. Recognizing these signs is akin to understanding the silent language of plants, allowing us to nurture them back to health.

SIGNS OF EMOTIONAL DISTRESS IN CHILDREN WITH A NARCISSISTIC PARENT

Children, in their resilience and adaptability, often find ways to cope with the complexities of having a narcissistic parent. Yet, the emotional toll often manifests in subtle and overt signs of distress. Spotting these signals early can open the door to providing the support and intervention necessary to foster healing and emotional growth.

Changes in Behavior or Mood

- **Withdrawal**: A once bubbly and outgoing child may become quiet and withdrawn, preferring solitude over the company of friends or family. This change might be a defense mechanism against the unpredictability of the narcissistic parent's attention or affection.

- **Aggression**: Frustration and confusion about their home dynamics can lead children to express their emotions through aggression. This might be more pronounced in environments where they feel safer, like at school or with the non-narcissistic parent.

- **Anxiety**: Constant tension at home, mainly due to walking on eggshells around a narcissistic parent, can lead to heightened anxiety in children. Signs include nail-biting, restlessness, or an unusual fear of making mistakes.

- **Depression**: Emotional neglect from a narcissistic parent can sow seeds of low self-esteem and sadness, displaying as a loss of interest in activities they once enjoyed, changes in appetite, or a pervasive sense of hopelessness.

Academic and Social Impact

- **Decline in School Performance**: The emotional burden of coping with a narcissistic parent can distract children from their studies, leading to a noticeable drop in academic performance.

- **Difficulties in Social Relationships**: Children may struggle to form and maintain friendships. They might either become overly pleasing, mirroring their home environment's dynamics or struggle with trust, fearing betrayal or rejection.

Physical Symptoms

- **Stress-Related Health Issues**: Chronic stress can manifest physically, presenting as recurrent headaches, stomachaches, or even unexplained aches and pains. These symptoms often lack a clear medical cause but are rooted in emotional distress.

- **Sleep Disturbances**: Difficulty falling asleep, nightmares, or excessive sleeping can all be indicators of underlying emotional turmoil stemming from the instability and unpredictability of living with a narcissistic parent.

Mimicking Narcissistic Behaviors

- **Imitating Behaviors**: Children often learn by example, and in some cases, they might start displaying narcissistic traits themselves, such as a lack of empathy or an inflated sense of entitlement. It's crucial to distinguish these learned behaviors from the child's character, understanding they stem from their environment rather than their nature.

Interactive Element: Reflection Journal Prompts

A series of guided journal prompts designed to help parents reflect on their child's behavior and mood changes. This exercise encourages a deeper understanding and awareness of the subtle signs of emotional distress, facilitating a proactive approach to seeking help and supporting the child.

- **Prompt 1**: Reflect on any significant changes in your child's behavior or mood in the past few months. What patterns do you notice?

- **Prompt 2**: How does your child express frustration or sadness? Are there specific triggers or patterns?

- **Prompt 3**: Think about your child's social interactions. Have you noticed any shifts in how they relate to friends or family members?

Recognizing the signs of emotional distress in children with a narcissistic parent is the first step toward intervention and support. Understanding and responding to these signs can pave the way for nurturing our children back to emotional health and well-being.

TEACHING RESILIENCE: STRATEGIES FOR SHIELDING CHILDREN EMOTIONALLY

In childhood development, resilience emerges as a vital attribute, weaving strength and adaptability into a child's character. When faced with the emotional complexities inherent in having a narcissistic parent, nurturing resilience in children becomes not merely beneficial but crucial. It gives them the psychological armor to withstand and recover from their challenges. Here, we explore practical strategies to fortify children emotionally, enabling them to navigate the ebbs and flows of their unique familial circumstances with confidence and poise.

Understanding the Foundation of Resilience

Resilience is not innate but a skill that children develop over time through experiences and guidance. It involves recognizing their inner strength, understanding that adversity is transient, and knowing they possess the agency to influence their outcomes. For children in the shadow of narcissistic parenting, resilience offers strength and hope, illuminating paths to emotional well-being and personal growth.

Cultivating Positive Self-Perception

The cornerstone of resilience is a positive self-perception. Children need to see themselves as capable and deserving individuals. This self-view counteracts any negative feedback they may receive from a narcissistic parent. Parents and caregivers can nurture this by:

- **Affirming their strengths**: Regularly acknowledge and celebrate the child's talents, efforts, and achievements. Highlight their unique qualities that contribute to their sense of self-worth.

- **Encouraging self-reflection**: Guide children to reflect on their experiences, focusing on what they learned and how they navigated challenges. This reflection fosters a growth mindset, emphasizing the value of effort and perseverance.

Fostering Emotional Literacy

Equipping children with the language to express their feelings allows them to articulate their experiences and seek support when needed. Emotional literacy is a tool for children to understand and manage their emotions effectively, a crucial aspect of resilience. Strategies include:

- **Naming emotions**: Use everyday situations to help children identify and name their feelings. This practice demystifies emotions, making them less overwhelming and more manageable.

- **Modeling emotional expression**: Demonstrate healthy ways to express emotions, such as talking about feelings openly or using art and play. This modeling teaches children that it's okay to express their feelings constructively.

Building a Support Network

A robust support network provides children with a safety net, reinforcing that they are not alone. This network can include family members, friends, teachers, and mentors who offer emotional and practical support. To build this network:

- **Encourage social connections**: Support children in developing friendships and participating in group activities that interest them. These connections can offer emotional support and a sense of belonging.

- **Connect with role models**: Introduce children to positive role models who have overcome adversity. These individuals can inspire children and provide tangible examples of resilience in action.

Teaching Problem-Solving Skills

Resilient children view challenges as opportunities for growth rather than insurmountable obstacles. Teaching children problem-solving skills empowers them to tackle difficulties with confidence. This can be achieved by:

- **Brainstorming solutions together**: When facing a problem, sit with the child and brainstorm potential solutions. Encourage creative thinking and evaluate the pros and cons of each option together.

- **Celebrating problem-solving attempts**: Recognize and praise the effort put into solving problems, regardless of the outcome. This recognition reinforces the value of trying and learning from the experience.

Promoting Autonomy and Decision-Making

Allowing children to make choices and experience the consequences of their decisions fosters a sense of autonomy. This independence is a critical component of resilience, as it instills confidence in their ability to influence their lives. Ways to promote autonomy include:

- **Offering controlled choices**: Provide children with options in matters that affect them, such as choosing extracurricular activities or setting weekend plans. This practice encourages them to weigh decisions and consider their preferences.

- **Supporting independence**: Encourage children to take on age-appropriate responsibilities and tasks, offering guidance as needed. This independence builds self-efficacy and a belief in their capabilities.

Prioritizing Self-Care and Wellness

Physical well-being significantly impacts emotional resilience. Ensuring children engage in regular physical activity, maintain a balanced diet, and get adequate sleep lays the foundation for emotional strength. Additionally, introducing children to mindfulness and relaxation techniques can help them manage stress and maintain emotional equilibrium.

Seeking Professional Support When Necessary

There are instances where professional support becomes an invaluable resource in building resilience. This may include counseling or therapy, which provides children with a safe space to process their emotions and experiences under the guidance of a trained professional. If signs of emotional distress persist or intensify, seeking professional help can offer the specialized guidance needed to navigate these challenges successfully.

Building resilience in children is a proactive journey that requires patience, understanding, and consistent effort. By implementing these strategies, parents and caregivers can equip children with the tools they need to face the complexities of life with a narcissistic parent with strength, adaptability, and a hopeful outlook on the future.

FOSTERING OPEN COMMUNICATION: TALKING TO KIDS ABOUT NARCISSISM

When the time arrives to discuss the intricacies of narcissism with our children, the approach must be tailored with care, adapting to their age and emotional maturity. This conversation, delicate yet necessary, aims not to vilify their narcissistic parent but to enlighten and empower our children, equipping them with understanding and coping strategies that respect their relationship with both parents.

Starting the Conversation

Initiating this dialogue requires timing and tact. Look for a moment of calm, free from recent conflicts, to ensure the discussion is as objective and unperturbed by emotion as possible. Begin by affirming your child's feelings and experiences, validating any confusion or hurt they might have encountered. This validation forms the bedrock of trust, essential for an open and honest conversation.

Explaining Narcissism in Accessible Terms

The concept of narcissism, complex even for adults, needs simplifying for a younger audience. Compare it to familiar situations or stories, perhaps likening it to characters from books or movies known for their self-centered behavior, to illustrate the traits without direct accusation or negativity. For older children, use examples from nature, such as the peacock, which always displays its feathers, to explain the need for attention and admiration that characterizes narcissism.

- **Younger Children**: "Sometimes, people can act like [character from a story], where they only talk about what they want and don't listen to others. It's not because they don't care, but they might not know how to show it properly."

- **Older Children**: "You know how a peacock always wants to show its feathers? Some people need a lot of attention like that. It doesn't mean they don't love us; they just express it differently and sometimes don't realize when we're upset or need something."

Addressing Their Feelings and Experiences

Encourage your children to share their feelings and experiences openly, reassuring them that all emotions are valid and that feeling confused or upset is okay. Use reflective listening to show that you truly hear and understand them, repeating what they've said in your own words and asking gentle questions to delve deeper into their thoughts.

- "It sounds like you're saying you feel left out when Dad/Mom talks only about what they like. That must be really hard."

- "How does it make you feel when you're trying to tell them something important, and they don't seem to listen?"

Providing Reassurance

It's crucial to reassure children that the narcissistic behaviors of their parent are not their fault, nor are they responsible for fixing them. If possible, highlight the parent's positive qualities to maintain a balanced view and prevent demonization.

- "Your Dad/Mom loves you a lot, even if sometimes their actions make it hard to see. We all show love in different ways, and it's okay to be upset about it sometimes."

- "Remember, how people act is about them, not about you. You're a fantastic kid, and you are not responsible for making adults feel better."

Equipping Them with Coping Strategies

Offer practical coping strategies that they can use when they feel overwhelmed or unnoticed by their narcissistic parent. Teach them simple techniques for self-soothing, like deep breathing or having a special 'safe space' they can go to when they need a moment alone. Encourage them to pursue interests and activities that make them happy, providing a healthy outlet for their emotions and a sense of achievement independent of their parent's attention.

- **Self-Soothing Techniques**: "When things get too much, try taking deep breaths, in and out, slowly. Imagine blowing up a big balloon with your worries and then letting it go."

- **Developing Interests**: "What's something you've always wanted to try? Doing things you love is important, especially when you're feeling sad or ignored. It's a way to remind yourself of the amazing person you are."

Normalizing Seeking Help

Normalize seeking help, whether talking to a trusted adult or a counselor or participating in support groups for kids going through similar experiences. Emphasize that asking for help is a sign of strength and wisdom, not a weakness.

- "Sometimes, talking to someone outside the family can help us make sense of things. It's like when you're learning something new in school and ask the teacher for help. It's smart to ask for guidance when we need it."

Continual Support and Open Doors

Conclude your discussion by reinforcing that this conversation isn't a one-time event but the beginning of an ongoing dialogue. Remind them that your door is always open for them to share their thoughts, feelings, and questions at any time.

- "What we talked about today is a lot to think about, and it's okay if you have more questions later on. Remember, I'm here for you, always ready to listen, whether you're feeling happy, sad, or anything in between."

In navigating these discussions, our goal is to shed light on the shadows cast by narcissism, offering our children the clarity, support, and love they need to understand their experiences and emotions. By fostering open communication, we lay the groundwork for healing and growth, ensuring our children feel seen, heard, and valued—no matter the circumstances.

THE IMPORTANCE OF EMOTIONAL INTELLIGENCE IN CHILDREN'S DEVELOPMENT

Emotional intelligence stands as an essential pillar in the foundation of a child's development, particularly when they are navigating the challenges posed by a parent's narcissistic tendencies. This capability enables them to recognize, understand, manage, and use emotions positively to relieve stress, communicate effectively, empathize with others, and overcome challenges. For children under the shadow of a narcissistic parent, developing emotional intelligence is not just beneficial; it's transformative, offering them tools to cope with complex emotional landscapes.

Recognizing and Naming Emotions

One of the first steps in cultivating emotional intelligence is teaching children to recognize and name their emotions. This skill allows them to identify what they are feeling at any moment, whether it's joy, sadness, anger, or fear. It's akin to giving them a map of a dense forest; with it, they can easily navigate the emotional underbrush.

- **Activities for Identification**: Simple games involving identifying emotions in others, such as through facial expressions in pictures, can be a fun way for children to become more attuned to their emotional states and those around them.

Understanding Emotions

Beyond recognizing emotions, children benefit from learning about the nature of emotions themselves — that they are normal, that everyone experiences them, and that they are temporary. This understanding can be exceptionally comforting to children dealing with the unpredictability of a narcissistic parent, as it provides a sense of normalcy and control.

- **Discussion Points**: Conversations about times when emotions felt overwhelming but eventually passed can help children understand the temporary nature of emotions. Reading stories together that deal with complex emotions and discussing the characters' feelings and outcomes can further deepen this understanding.

Managing Emotions

Arguably, one of the most crucial aspects of emotional intelligence is learning to manage emotions effectively. For a child in a challenging co-parenting situation, the ability to calm themselves when upset or express their feelings constructively can be empowering. It allows them to cope with their immediate emotional environment and build resilience for the future.

- **Techniques for Management**: Teaching children simple breathing exercises or giving them a quiet space where they can go to calm down can be effective strategies. Encouraging them to articulate their feelings through words, art, or music can also provide an outlet for emotional expression.

Using Emotions Positively

Teaching children to use their emotions positively can encourage empathy, improve communication, and foster relationships. Understanding their feelings can help children anticipate and manage their reactions in social situations, including those involving a narcissistic parent, making interactions less stressful and more productive.

- **Role-Playing**: Engaging in role-playing scenarios where children can practice responding to different emotional situations can prepare them for real-life interactions. This practice can help them think about using their emotions to communicate more effectively and empathize with others.

Developing Empathy

Empathy, a core component of emotional intelligence, involves understanding and sharing the feelings of others. For children, developing empathy can improve their social interactions and offer a counterpoint to the self-centered behavior they may observe in a narcissistic parent. It teaches them to consider the perspectives and feelings of others, enriching their social and emotional worlds.

- **Modeling Empathy**: Parents can model empathy by expressing concern for others and discussing feelings in everyday situations. Asking children how they think someone else feels in a particular situation and why can help develop this skill.

Encouraging Effective Communication

Children with high emotional intelligence are often better communicators. They can express their needs and feelings clearly and constructively resolve conflicts. Given the communication challenges that can arise in families with a narcissistic parent, equipping children with these skills is invaluable.

- **Communication Skills Practice**: Activities that involve describing emotions and practicing active listening can enhance children's communication skills. Encouraging them to express themselves, ask questions, and listen carefully to others' responses can improve their communication ability.

Supporting Problem-Solving

Problem-solving is another area where emotional intelligence can benefit children, especially in complex family dynamics. Understanding their own and others' emotions can help children navigate disputes more effectively, finding solutions that consider everyone's feelings and needs.

- **Problem-Solving Exercises**: Working together on problem-solving exercises, where children are encouraged to identify the problem, consider everyone's feelings, and propose solutions, can build this skill. This approach helps with immediate family challenges and prepares children for handling conflicts in broader social contexts.

In nurturing emotional intelligence, children gain a set of skills and understandings that not only assist them in managing the immediate challenges of living with a narcissistic parent but also enrich their social and emotional lives into adulthood. Children can navigate their world with confidence and empathy by recognizing, understanding, managing, and using emotions effectively, building stronger, healthier relationships with themselves and others.

MODELING HEALTHY BOUNDARIES FOR CHILDREN

In households graced with the presence of a narcissistic parent, the art of boundary-setting transforms into a crucial skill akin to learning a new language—one that speaks of respect, self-worth, and mutual understanding. For children in this situation, witnessing boundary-setting in action serves as a powerful lesson, equipping them with tools to interact confidently with the world around them, including the challenging dynamics presented by a narcissistic parent.

Boundaries, at its core, revolve around understanding where one person ends and another begins—what behaviors are acceptable and what crosses the line. It's about recognizing one's own needs and ensuring they're met in healthy, respectful ways. This understanding begins in the home through observation and practice for children.

Instilling the Basics of Boundary Setting

To start, children benefit from seeing boundaries respected within their own family unit. As a parent, you want to lead by example and model the behavior you want to see in your children. Doing so involves simple, everyday actions:

- Respecting privacy: Knocking before entering their room, for instance, reinforces the concept of personal space.

- Valuing opinions: Allowing children to express their preferences and choices in matters that concern them teaches them their voice matters.

- Encouraging autonomy: Supporting children in doing tasks independently fosters a sense of self-reliance and personal responsibility.

Navigating Boundaries with a Narcissistic Parent

The unique challenge of setting boundaries with a narcissistic parent lies in the unpredictability and, often, the disregard for personal limits. Let's face it: narcissists do not recognize that other people, including their children, have boundaries, and this is a huge issue. This gives you, the stable parent, the opportunity to play a pivotal role in modeling boundary-setting:

- Demonstrating assertiveness: Showing children how to assert their needs respectfully and firmly gives them a script to follow in their interactions.

- Responding to overstepping: Calmly addressing instances when boundaries are crossed without resorting to anger or retaliation sets an example of handling conflicts constructively.

- Maintaining consistency: Upholding established boundaries, even in the face of resistance, illustrates the importance of consistency in healthy relationships.

The Role of Positive Reinforcement

Acknowledging and praising children when they set boundaries themselves fortifies these behaviors. Whether it's saying no to something they're uncomfortable with or asking for personal space, recognizing their efforts reinforces the value of boundaries. This positive reinforcement encourages them to continue asserting their needs and respecting others.

Creating a Safe Space for Practice

Home should be a sanctuary where children feel safe to explore and practice boundary-setting. Engaging in role-play scenarios, for instance, allows children to experiment with setting boundaries in a controlled, supportive environment. Discussions about hypothetical situations—how to say no to unwanted demands and ask for help—provide children with a toolkit of responses ready for real-life applications.

The Ripple Effect of Healthy Boundaries

The lessons learned from modeling healthy boundaries extend beyond immediate family dynamics. Children who understand and respect boundaries grow into adults who confidently and empathetically navigate social, academic, and professional relationships. They're equipped to handle challenges with resilience, understanding their rights, and respecting those of others.

In essence, the gift of boundary-setting is one of the most valuable legacies a parent can pass on to their children. It's a tool that empowers children to protect their well-being, advocate for their needs, and engage with others in a manner grounded in mutual respect and understanding. As we wrap up this exploration into the impact of narcissism on families and the power of resilience, emotional intelligence, and boundary-setting, we're reminded of the broader implications of these lessons. They're not just strategies for coping but foundational skills that shape how children view themselves and interact with the world.

Next, we look into the practicalities of establishing and maintaining these boundaries, navigating the intricacies of co-parenting with a narcissist, and fostering environments where children can thrive despite these challenges.

Chapter 3

Crafting Communication with Care

I n the dance of co-parenting with a narcissistic ex, mastering the steps of communication can feel more like navigating a minefield blindfolded. Each word, each pause, and each response holds the potential to either diffuse tension or escalate conflict. In this delicate balance, the Grey Rock Method emerges as the best strategy, offering a way to engage without igniting the flames of narcissistic supply. This chapter peels back the layers of this approach, guiding you through the nuanced art of communicating in ways that maintain peace and protect emotional well-being.

IMPLEMENTING THE GREY ROCK METHOD SAFELY

The Grey Rock Method: An Overview

Imagine for a moment a grey rock: unremarkable, uninteresting, blending into the background. It is now your goal, when dealing with your narcissistic ex, to become the emotional equivalent of a grey rock. This is the essence of the Grey Rock Method—becoming emotionally unresponsive, dull, and as unengaging as possible to avoid becoming a target of manipulation or conflict. It's not about becoming passive but rather choosing when and how to engage in a way that preserves your emotional energy. It is a communication style you must learn to get to the other side of all of this. You must not allow your narcissistic ex to see you react; you must not engage reactively. You must remain indifferent (outwardly) and be the grey rock. If the narcissist sees you react, it excites, encourages, and feeds their toxic behavior. They are bored and lose interest if you remain outwardly unaffected by their actions.

When to Use the Grey Rock Method

The Grey Rock Method shines in its ability to minimize emotional engagement in situations where direct communication can lead to conflict or emotional harm. It is particularly useful in conversations that are:

- Prone to escalation over minor issues.

- Centered around topics where the narcissistic ex seeks to provoke or extract a specific emotional response.

- Repeated attempts by the narcissist to draw you into unnecessary drama.

It's not a one-size-fits-all solution, nor is it meant for every interaction. Its power lies in selective application, especially in scenarios where engaging emotionally offers no benefit and only serves to fuel the narcissist's behaviors.

How to Implement the Grey Rock Method

Implementing this method involves a conscious choice of non-engagement on an emotional level while maintaining necessary communication about co-parenting responsibilities. This will require practice on your part. Here's how to do it effectively:

- **Keep responses brief and factual**: When discussing co-parenting logistics, stick to the facts. If asked a question, provide a direct, concise answer without elaboration.

- **Avoid personal topics**: Steer clear of discussions about personal life, feelings, or anything that isn't directly related to co-parenting duties. If such issues arise, politely redirect the conversation to the matter.

- **Maintain a neutral tone**: Use a calm, even tone of voice. Emotional reactions, whether positive or negative, can encourage further probing or manipulation attempts.

- **Practice detachment**: Before communicating, take a moment to prepare yourself to remain detached mentally. Visualize yourself as an observer rather than a participant in any emotional drama.

Challenges and Considerations

While the Grey Rock Method can be an effective tool, it has challenges. It requires practice and patience to master, and there may be times when it feels counterintuitive to withhold emotional responses. Additionally, it's important to monitor this method's impact on you. Consistently engaging in emotional detachment, especially with someone you once shared a close relationship with, can be draining.

It's also crucial to consider the children's perspectives. They shouldn't feel a lack of warmth or emotional support from you due to implementing this method. Balancing the Grey Rock Method in interactions with your ex while ensuring your children receive the emotional engagement they need from you is critical.

Interactive Element: Self-Reflection Exercise

Staying calm and not reacting when something outrageous comes up is hard; very hard. Writing down your feelings and experiences immediately after implementing the grey rock method can be very helpful. It will allow you a space to react and express your anger, anxiety, and frustration.

The following prompts may help you to reflect and process your experiences using the Grey Rock Method:

- "In what situations did I find the Grey Rock Method most effective?"

- "How did I feel before, during, and after using the Grey Rock Method?"

- "What challenges did I face in remaining emotionally detached, and how can I address them in the future?"

Navigating co-parenting with a narcissistic ex demands a careful, considered approach to communication. The Grey Rock Method, when used judiciously, offers a way to engage without exacerbating conflict, preserving your emotional well-being in the process. Yet, it's just one tool in the broader strategy of managing interactions with a narcissist. As we move forward, we'll explore additional techniques and approaches to fortify your communication arsenal, ensuring you're prepared to handle the challenges of co-parenting with calm, clarity, and confidence.

ESTABLISHING AND MAINTAINING BOUNDARIES THROUGH COMMUNICATION

In the intricate dynamics of co-parenting with a narcissistic ex, setting boundaries is not merely a strategy; it's a foundational pillar that upholds the structure of healthy interaction. Clear boundaries are absolutely necessary; they are non-negotiable. Now, we will look at how to make, set, and enforce healthy boundaries that foster a respectful and manageable co-parenting relationship.

The Framework of Boundaries

Boundaries in communication serve as invisible lines defining acceptable interaction limits. They are the parameters within which healthy dialogue flourishes and toxic overreach is curtailed. To establish these, you must first identify what behaviors are acceptable and which are not. This clarity is paramount. It could range from the tone of voice used in conversations to the topics that are off-limits or the frequency of communication. You should take your time and come up with an exhaustive list.

The Initial Conversation

The first step in boundary-setting involves communicating these limits to the narcissistic ex. This conversation should be planned with a clear, calm mindset and agenda. Make sure you are well prepared and organized before entering into this conversation. It is a good idea to have things written out to ensure you make your expectations clear. Begin by affirming the shared goal of prioritizing the children's well-being. Then, articulate the boundaries you are setting, why they are necessary, and how they benefit co-parenting efforts. It's crucial here to speak from a place of "I" statements, such as "I feel" or "I need," to own your boundaries without placing blame.

Consistency Is Key

The test of boundaries lies in their maintenance. Narcissistic individuals will almost always test these limits repeatedly; thus, consistency in enforcing them is crucial. If a boundary is crossed, refer to the initial conversation and the agreed-upon limits. Again, it would help if you had these boundaries written down as a reference for both parties. Consistent reinforcement through calm, firm responses solidifies these boundaries over time.

Adjustments and Flexibility

While consistency is crucial, so too is adaptability. Life's unpredictability may necessitate adjustments to previously set boundaries. When changes are needed, approach them with the same clarity and respect as the initial boundary-setting conversation. Explain the reasons for adjustments and remain open to dialogue, ensuring the changes continue to serve the children's best interests.

Strategies for Boundary Communication

- **Scheduled Updates**: Establish regular intervals for discussing co-parenting matters, reducing the need for constant back-and-forth communication.

- **Written Agreements**: Having a written record of agreed-upon boundaries provides a precise reference point for both parties, useful for clarifying disputes.

- **Neutral Spaces**: Choosing a neutral setting for discussions about boundaries can reduce the emotional charge, making it easier to focus on the issues.

Handling Pushback

Resistance is a typical response, especially from a narcissistic ex, when new boundaries are set. When faced with pushback, remain calm and redirect the conversation to the primary focus: the well-being of the children. Having a mediator present during these discussions may be beneficial to maintain focus and neutrality.

Self-Care and Support

Setting and maintaining boundaries with a narcissistic ex can be emotionally taxing. Prioritizing self-care and seeking support from friends, family, or professionals can provide the emotional resilience needed for this task. Remember, setting boundaries is not just about creating a healthier co-parenting environment; it's also about preserving your well-being. Dealing with a narcissist is incredibly draining; make sure you are prioritizing your self-care. You need to be strong to advocate for your children.

The Role of Empathy

While it may seem counterintuitive, empathy can be a valuable tool in boundary-setting with a narcissistic ex. Understanding their perspective (without condoning inappropriate behavior) can inform more effective communication strategies. For instance, recognizing a desire for control may lead to offering limited choices rather than open-ended questions, satisfying their need for influence while protecting core boundaries.

The Children's Perspective

Consider the impact on the children in all discussions and strategies around boundary-setting. They should never be in the middle of boundary disputes. Instead, communicate the importance of these boundaries in creating a stable, predictable environment for them. This protects the children and models healthy communication and boundary-setting practices they can carry into their relationships.

Empowering children with age-appropriate discussions about boundaries can also offer them a sense of security and control. Teach them they have the right to set personal boundaries and how to communicate these respectfully.

In sum, establishing and maintaining boundaries in communication with a narcissistic ex is a delicate, ongoing process that requires clarity, consistency, and a commitment to the well-being of all involved. Through careful planning, empathetic understanding, and steadfast reinforcement, it's possible to create a co-parenting dynamic that respects individual needs while prioritizing the health and happiness of the children at its heart.

TECHNIQUES FOR NEUTRAL, FACT BASED EXCHANGES

In the landscape of co-parenting with a narcissistic ex, the path to peaceful and productive communication often lies in the terrain of neutral, fact-based exchanges. This
method emphasizes the importance of sticking to the facts, avoiding emotional language,
and maintaining a neutral tone. It's a strategy designed to reduce conflict and foster a
co-parenting environment where misunderstandings are minimized, and the children's
well-being is at the forefront.

The Foundation of Fact-Based Communication

Fact-based communication distills conversations to the essential information required for
effective co-parenting. This approach involves:

- Discussing schedules, logistics, and children's needs without personal commen-
  tary.

- Sharing relevant updates about the children's health, education, and well-being
  succinctly.

- Making requests or changes to co-parenting arrangements in a direct, unambiguous manner.

This method doesn't eliminate the need for empathy or understanding; instead, it streamlines communication to focus on co-parenting responsibilities, sidelining potential triggers for conflict.

Strategies for Maintaining Neutrality

Maintaining a neutral tone might not always come intuitively, especially in emotionally
charged situations. However, several strategies can facilitate this approach:

- **Preparation**: Before initiating communication, take a moment to outline the
  points you need to cover. This helps in staying on track and avoiding detours
  into emotional territory.

- **Pause Before Responding**: If a message from your ex-partner evokes an emotional reaction, give yourself time to process these feelings separately before crafting your response. This pause can prevent the escalation of emotions.

- **Mindful Language**: Choose words carefully to avoid unintentional provocation. Phrases that begin with "I noticed" or "I observed" can introduce facts without implying blame or judgment.

Examples of Neutral Exchanges

To visualize how neutral, fact-based exchanges unfold, consider these examples:

- Instead of saying, "You always return the kids late on your weekends," try. "The agreed-upon time for returning the kids is 7 PM. Let's ensure this is followed to maintain their routine."

- Replace "You never inform me about the parent-teacher meetings" with "Both of us must be informed about the parent-teacher meetings. Let's update each other moving forward."

These reframed statements focus on the issue at hand, devoid of accusatory language, paving the way for constructive dialogue.

The Role of Written Communication

In many cases, written communication is ideal for neutral exchanges. It allows time for thought and revision, ensuring the message remains focused and factual. Furthermore, written records can be invaluable in maintaining clarity and accountability over agreements and discussions. This is where the co-parenting apps can be a huge help and asset. When opting for written communication:

- **Emails and Texts**: Utilize these for scheduling, updates, and non-urgent matters, keeping the language clear and to the point.

- **Online Co-Parenting Tools**: Platforms designed for co-parenting can streamline communication, providing structured ways to share information, schedule changes, and financial management, all while focusing on the children's needs.

Navigating Difficult Topics

Even with a commitment to neutrality, certain topics may inherently carry emotional weight. In these situations:

- **Acknowledge Emotions Without Dwelling on Them**: Recognize that some discussions may evoke feelings but reiterate the need to resolve the matter constructively.

- **Seek External Support if Needed**: For topics that repeatedly lead to conflict, consider involving a neutral third party, such as a mediator or a GAL, to facilitate the discussion.

Feedback and Reevaluation

Effective communication is a dynamic process requiring ongoing adjustment and feedback. Periodically, take time to:

- **Assess the Effectiveness**: Reflect on recent exchanges to identify what's working and what isn't. This can involve personal reflection or feedback from trusted advisors.

- **Adjust as Needed**: Be willing to try different approaches or communication methods if certain strategies are not yielding the desired outcomes. Flexibility can lead to discovering more effective ways to communicate.

By embracing neutral, fact-based exchanges, co-parents can create a communication landscape that focuses on effectively raising their children together. This approach minimizes the emotional friction often encountered in co-parenting with a narcissistic ex, fostering a more harmonious and constructive co-parenting relationship.

UTILIZING TECHNOLOGY TO MANAGE COMMUNICATION AND MINIMIZE CONTACT

In the digital age, technology emerges as a powerful ally in navigating the complexities of co-parenting with a narcissistic ex. The strategic use of digital tools streamlines the necessary exchange of information and reduces the need for direct, potentially conflict-laden contact. This section explores how various technological solutions can be leveraged to foster a more manageable and less emotionally charged co-parenting environment.

Digital Platforms for Co-Parenting

A plethora of dedicated co-parenting applications exist today, designed with the specific aim of facilitating communication between separated parents. These platforms are centralized hubs where you can schedule appointments, share important documents, update educational information, and track expenses without direct interaction. Using these tools, you create a documented communication trail, which can be invaluable in maintaining clarity and accountability. Some notable features include:

- **Shared Calendars**: These allow for the visualization of the children's schedules, making it easier to coordinate between households. It will also ensure that each parent knows the days and times of children's activities. Many shared calendars are available, two of the most popular being an Apple or Google calendar.

- **Document Storage**: Vital records such as medical reports, school reports, and extracurricular schedules can be uploaded for shared access, ensuring both parents have the necessary information at their fingertips. There are several platforms available for this. Dropbox is very popular, and in cases of high conflict, parents may prefer to use an app like Our Family Wizard or Talking Parents.

- **Expense Tracking**: Many apps offer features to record and manage shared expenses, streamlining the process and reducing disputes over financial contributions.

Apps for Co-Parenting:

There are many apps available. Please do your own research to find the app best suited for your specific needs. Below are some of the most popular apps on the market, but there are many to choose from.

Recommended for High-Conflict Co-Parenting and Parallel Parenting:

Our Family Wizard www.ourfamilywizard.com

Court-approved and recommended by many family law practices. Everything is time-stamped, and nothing can be deleted.

The main features include a shared calendar, video calls and traditional calls, messages, expenses, an important information vault, a journal for documenting anything that comes up, and a tone meter to keep all communications civil.

Talking Parents www.talkingparents.com

The main features include accountable calling, secure messaging, unalterable records, shared calendar accountable payments, an info library, a personal journal, and an attachment library.

Other Highly recommended apps:

2Houses www.2houses.com

The main features include a shared calendar, information vault, finance tracker, and journal.

Appclose www.appclose.com

The main features include a shared calendar, a secure message center where messages cannot be deleted, a request center, audio and video calls, and an expense center.

CoParenter www.coparenter.com

The main features include mediation, check-ins, a shared calendar, and records.

Selective Messaging Services

Selective messaging services offer an alternative for parents who prefer not to use a dedicated co-parenting app. Email or specific messaging apps can be designated solely for co-parenting communication. This approach allows for the following:

- **Filtered Communication**: By dedicating a specific platform for co-parenting discussions, you can more easily maintain a professional tone and keep the conversation focused on the children's needs.

- **Documented Interactions**: Like co-parenting apps, these services record all exchanges, which can help resolve misunderstandings or provide evidence of agreements.

Creating a Communication Protocol

To maximize the benefits of technology in co-parenting, it's helpful to establish a communication protocol. This agreement outlines which platforms will be used, the types of information to be shared through each, and guidelines for response times. When possible, crafting this protocol together with your ex-partner can ensure mutual understanding and compliance. It is also beneficial if your lawyer and/or GAL helps to negotiate this. Key considerations include:

- **Choosing the Right Tools**: Decide together on the most suitable apps or services based on your specific co-parenting needs.

- **Setting Expectations**: Agree on reasonable expectations for how quickly messages should be acknowledged and responded to.

- **Emergency Plans**: Outline how and when to communicate in emergencies, ensuring that both parents are promptly informed.

The Role of Privacy Settings

Privacy and security should be considered when utilizing technology for co-parent communication. Ensure that all chosen platforms have robust privacy settings and that personal data is protected. This includes:

- **Password Protection**: Use strong, unique passwords for all co-parenting platforms and services.

- **Privacy Settings**: Familiarize yourself with and adjust the privacy settings on each platform to safeguard your information.

- **Secure Document Sharing**: When sharing sensitive documents, use encryption and secure access services.

Encouraging Children's Input

As children grow older, their input on co-parenting arrangements becomes increasingly valuable. Technology can facilitate their involvement in a way that respects their autonomy while keeping both parents informed. For instance:

- **Inclusion in Scheduling**: Older children can be given access to view the shared calendar, allowing them to stay informed and, when appropriate, voice their preferences or concerns.

- **Direct Communication Channels**: Establishing a safe, direct line of communication between the children and each parent ensures they can reach out when they need support, advice, or to share their day.

In leveraging technology to manage co-parenting communication, the goal is to create an environment where logistical and informational needs are met efficiently and respectfully. Minimizing direct contact reduces the potential for conflict and emotional strain, paving the way for a more harmonious co-parenting relationship. It's a strategy that benefits the parents and provides the children with a sense of stability and peace, knowing that their well-being is the priority guiding these choices.

HANDLING MANIPULATIVE COMMUNICATION: DO'S AND DONT'S

In the realm of co-parenting with a narcissistic ex, one often encounters communication laced with manipulative intents. Identifying and navigating these attempts is not merely beneficial; it's vital for maintaining a sense of equilibrium and safeguarding the emotional environment for both you and your children.

Manipulative communication can take various forms, from guilt-tripping to gaslighting, and often aims to unsettle you, question your perceptions, or coerce you into compliance. Recognizing these tactics is the first step towards disarming them. Here are practical do's and don'ts for handling manipulative communication, designed to equip you with the necessary tools to respond confidently and clearly.

Recognize the Signs of Manipulation

Before diving into strategies, it's crucial to recognize manipulation. Signs include attempts to elicit guilt, shifting blame, twisting facts, or playing the victim. When you sense these patterns emerging, it's a signal to proceed cautiously and employ the strategies outlined below.

Do's

- **Stay Focused on the Issue**: When discussions veer into manipulative territory, gently steer the conversation back to the core issue. This focus helps prevent getting drawn into emotional whirlpools that distract from resolving co-parenting matters.

- **Respond, Don't React**: Give yourself permission to take a step back and respond thoughtfully rather than reacting impulsively. This space allows you to assess the situation and decide on the most constructive action.

- **Seek Clarification**: If you suspect manipulation, asking for clarification can be powerful. It forces the other party to explain their statements more clearly, often revealing the manipulative intent or confusion behind them.

- **Use "I" Statements**: Expressing your thoughts and feelings using "I" statements can help you take ownership of your responses and reduce defensive reactions from your co-parent.

- **Document Suspicious Interactions**: Keeping a record of interactions that felt manipulative can be helpful for personal reflection, understanding patterns, and, if necessary, for legal purposes.

- **Use Co-Parenting App**: Using a co-parenting app will document all communication, and in apps such as Our Family Wizard, there is even a mechanism to detect the tone of the communications sent. This can go a long way in keeping the peace and eliminate your ex's manipulation ability.

Don'ts

- **Engage in Tit-for-Tat**: Avoid the temptation to respond to manipulative tactics with manipulation of your own. This approach only escalates conflicts and detracts from productive resolution. Whenever possible and as much as possible, take the high road. Before you send a text or email, ask yourself: how would I feel if my children read this? How would I feel if the family court read this?

- **Ignore Your Instincts**: If something feels off, trust your instincts. Dismissing your gut feelings can lead to overlooking manipulative behaviors that might otherwise be addressed.

- **Get Drawn into Emotional Arguments**: Manipulative communication often aims to provoke an emotional reaction. Resist the urge to engage in arguments that are emotionally charged and unproductive. Utilize the Grey Rock Method.

- **Over-Explain or Justify**: Offering excessive explanations or justifications for your decisions or feelings can give manipulative individuals more leverage to argue or twist your words. Keep explanations concise and rooted in facts.

- **Forget to Prioritize Self-Care**: Handling manipulative communication can be draining. Prioritizing self-care is essential for maintaining the emotional strength needed to navigate these interactions effectively.

Handling manipulative communication effectively requires awareness, self-control, and strategic response. By implementing these do's and don'ts, you can better manage the challenges of co-parenting with a narcissistic ex, fostering a healthier communication environment for both you and your children.

As we close this chapter, the strategies presented offer a roadmap for navigating the often tumultuous waters of co-parenting with a narcissistic partner. From embracing the Grey Rock Method to implementing clear boundaries, maintaining neutral exchanges, leveraging technology, and handling manipulative communication, each tool protects your emotional well-being and promotes a more harmonious co-parenting relationship. As we move forward, remember that the ultimate goal remains the same: ensuring the well-being and happiness of your children while navigating the complexities of co-parenting with strength, resilience, and clarity.

Chapter 4

Legal Frameworks and Financial Stability: Navigating the Maze

S tepping into the legal and financial aspects of co-parenting with a narcissistic ex can feel like navigating a maze designed without an exit in sight. The twists and turns, dead ends, and occasional surprises can leave you feeling lost and overwhelmed. Yet, with the right map and compass—in the form of knowledge and strategies—the path becomes more apparent, and the journey, though challenging, leads to a place of empowerment and security for both you and your children.

DOCUMENTING NARCISSISTIC BEHAVIOR FOR LEGAL PURPOSES

In the context of legal disputes, the pen indeed proves mightier than the sword. Documenting instances of narcissistic behavior and its impact on co-parenting isn't about keeping a scorecard of wrongs but about having a factual base to support your case in court or mediation sessions. It's about presenting an objective, fact-based account for the legal system, which relies heavily on tangible evidence to make informed decisions.

Why Documentation Matters

Evidence is critical in any legal dispute, especially those involving custody or co-parenting arrangements. The court's primary concern is the well-being of the children involved, and decisions are made based on what arrangement serves their best interests. Documenting instances of manipulative, neglectful, or abusive behavior by a narcissistic ex-partner can underscore concerns about their parenting capabilities and the impact on the children. Being able to provide the court with a well-documented paper trail of abusive, manipulative, inciteful text messages and/or emails is very helpful.

What to Document

- **Direct Interactions**: Keep records of all forms of communication, including texts, emails, and notes from phone calls, especially those that showcase manipulative tactics, refusal to co-parent effectively, or direct impact on the children.

- **Behavioral Patterns**: Note dates and details of any actions demonstrating a lack of cooperation in co-parenting, failure to adhere to agreed-upon parenting plans, or instances where the narcissistic behavior directly affected the children.

- **Children's Responses**: Observations of changes in the children's behavior or emotional state following interactions with the narcissistic parent can be significant. This might include signs of stress, anxiety, or reluctance to spend time with the other parent.

How to Organize Documentation

- **Chronological Logs**: Maintain a diary or log in chronological order. This makes it easier to reference specific instances and shows patterns over time. Keeping these records using an app or software that will time-stamp entries and prevent messages from being edited and/or deleted is helpful.

- **Electronic Records**: Utilize digital tools and apps designed for record-keeping. Many offer date-stamped entries and the ability to upload screenshots or photos, providing a secure and organized way to store documentation. This is the best way to ensure an objective, verifiable record of interactions.

Legal Considerations

Before recording conversations to document behavior, it's crucial to understand the legalities involved. Laws regarding recording conversations vary by location, and actions perceived as invasive could potentially harm your case. Consult with a legal professional to ensure your documentation methods are legally sound and will be admissible in court.

Documenting narcissistic behavior for legal purposes requires a systematic and informed approach. Again, asking the court to appoint a GAL can be exceptionally helpful. GALs have seen and dealt with narcissistic parents before and can quickly see the situation clearly. By systematically recording relevant interactions and behaviors, you build a foundation of evidence that can support your case, highlighting concerns for your children's well-being and ensuring their interests are protected in legal proceedings. Again, before recording any conversations check with an attorney to confirm that this is legal; if it is not legal, do not record any conversations. It's a proactive step towards establishing a co-parenting arrangement that prioritizes your children's safety and emotional health, providing them with the stable and nurturing environment they deserve.

STRATEGIES FOR MANAGING FINANCES AND CHILD SUPPORT ISSUES

Financial disputes often present a significant challenge in the realm of co-parenting, especially when one party exhibits narcissistic traits. The manipulation of finances and child support can serve as a tool for control, creating a complex web of challenges that require strategic navigation. To manage these intricacies effectively, a multi-faceted approach is necessary, ensuring the financial stability of the co-parenting arrangement while safeguarding the well-being of all involved parties.

Understanding Financial Manipulation

At the outset, it's crucial to recognize the signs of financial manipulation. This could range from delaying child support payments as a means to exert control to extravagant spending during visitation to win the child's affection, overshadowing the more measured financial contributions of the other parent. Recognizing these tactics is the first step in countering them, setting the stage for a more balanced and less contentious financial co-parenting dynamic.

Securing a Clear Child Support Agreement

A legally binding child support agreement forms the cornerstone of a stable financial arrangement. This agreement should detail the amount, frequency, and method of child support payments, considering the child's needs and both parents' financial capabilities. Working with legal professionals to draft this agreement is advisable, ensuring it's comprehensive and enforceable.

- **Legal Documentation**: Ensure all agreements are documented and legalized to prevent future discrepancies or disputes.

- **Adjustments Over Time**: Acknowledge that the child's needs and parents' financial situations can change, necessitating adjustments to the agreement. Include provisions for periodic reviews and modifications.

Implementing Financial Tracking

Accurate tracking of child support payments and related expenses is vital. It provides a transparent record to help resolve disputes and uphold financial responsibilities.

- **Use of Financial Apps**: Numerous apps are designed to track child support payments, medical expenses, educational costs, and other child-related expenditures. These tools can simplify record-keeping and provide easy access to financial data for both parents.

- **Receipts and Invoices**: Maintain a file of receipts, invoices, and other documentation related to child-related expenses. This practice is beneficial for both record-keeping and tax purposes. Many parenting apps mentioned in this book have the functionality to allow you to upload receipts and track expenses.

Creating a Budget for Child-Related Expenses

A well-structured budget for child-related expenses lays a clear foundation for financial planning. It helps anticipate future costs and ensures that both parents contribute fairly to their child's upbringing.

- **Collaborative Planning**: Whenever possible, involve the other parent in budget planning. Doing so can help in aligning expectations and responsibilities.

- **Emergency Fund**: Consider setting aside an emergency fund for unforeseen child-related expenses. This can alleviate financial stress and prevent last-minute conflicts over unexpected costs.

Dealing with Delays and Non-Payment

Despite a clear and explicit agreement, there might be instances of delayed payments or non-compliance. In dealing with narcissists, it is not uncommon for them to use finance and child support payments as a weapon, so prepare yourself. Handling these situations requires a blend of patience and assertiveness.

- **Direct Communication**: Initially, address the issue directly with the other parent. A respectful reminder about the agreement and its importance to the child's well-being might resolve temporary lapses.

- **Legal Enforcement**: If non-compliance persists, legal mechanisms exist to enforce child support agreements. Familiarize yourself with these processes and, if necessary, seek legal counsel to pursue enforcement.

Financial Independence and Self-Reliance

While child support is essential, cultivating financial independence and self-reliance adds an extra layer of security. This isn't about diminishing the other parent's financial responsibilities but ensuring stability regardless of the co-parenting dynamic.

- **Income Diversification**: Explore opportunities for income diversification. This could include additional job opportunities, side projects, or investments.

- **Financial Education**: Invest in your financial education. Understanding budgeting, savings, investments, and financial planning strengthens your ability to manage finances confidently and independently.

Navigating the financial terrain of co-parenting with a narcissistic ex-partner demands a strategic, informed approach. By establishing clear agreements, maintaining meticulous financial records, and fostering an environment of financial education and independence, you can create a stable foundation supporting your children's well-being and future.

This reinforces the importance of resilience, communication, and proactive planning in securing a financially stable and harmonious co-parenting arrangement.

NAVIGATING CUSTODY AGREEMENTS WITH A NARCISSISTIC EX

Crafting a custody agreement when one party exhibits narcissistic traits demands a nuanced approach. The primary focus must always be on the welfare of the children, ensuring their needs are met in a stable environment. Here, we explore strategies to create a balanced agreement, emphasizing the importance of legal guidance throughout the process.

Preparation Is Key

Thorough preparation can make a significant difference before entering negotiations or court proceedings. This includes:

- **Understanding Your Rights**: Familiarize yourself with your legal rights and obligations regarding custody in your jurisdiction. Knowledge is power, and understanding the legal framework sets a solid foundation for the discussions ahead.

- **Prioritizing Children's Needs**: Clearly outline what arrangements will best support your children's physical, emotional, and educational needs. This might involve considerations around their schooling, extracurricular activities, and emotional support systems.

- **Anticipating Challenges**: Given the nature of narcissistic behavior, anticipate potential objections or manipulations from your ex-partner. Preparing for these challenges allows you to address them more effectively when they arise.

Seeking Legal Guidance

The complexity of negotiating custody with a narcissistic ex often necessitates professional legal advice. A family law attorney can provide:

- **Expertise**: A lawyer experienced in handling high-conflict custody cases can offer invaluable advice tailored to your specific situation.

- **Advocacy**: In court, your lawyer acts as your advocate, articulating your case clearly and effectively to support the best interests of your children.

- **Mediation Support**: Lawyers can also facilitate or recommend professional mediators skilled in resolving disputes between parents, potentially avoiding the need for court altogether.

Structuring the Agreement

When drafting the custody agreement, certain elements can help in managing the co-parenting relationship with a narcissistic ex:

- **Detailed Provisions**: The more specific the agreement, the less room for manipulation or misinterpretation. Include detailed schedules, holiday arrangements, and provisions for communication.

- **Flexibility Clauses**: While specificity is crucial, including clauses that allow for adjustments as children grow and their needs change can prevent future conflicts.

- **Parallel Parenting Considerations**: In situations where cooperative co-parenting is unfeasible, parallel parenting arrangements allow each parent to have independent relationships with their children, minimizing direct contact between the parents. This can be especially true in cases where your ex is a narcissist. (Parallel Parenting will be explained in the next chapter)

Communication Strategies

Effective communication is vital in negotiating and implementing a custody agreement. Strategies include:

- **Written Proposals**: Presenting your custody suggestions in writing provides a precise reference point for discussions and negotiations.

- **Neutral Language**: Use objective, neutral language in all communications to reduce potential conflict.

- **Documented Exchanges**: Keep a record of all communications regarding custody arrangements. This documentation can be crucial in resolving disputes or misunderstandings.

Protecting Well-Being

Protecting your and your children's emotional well-being is paramount throughout the custody negotiation process. Strategies to consider:

- **Self-Care Practices**: Engage in regular self-care activities to manage stress and maintain your emotional resilience.

- **Support Systems**: Lean on your support network of friends, family, and professionals for emotional and practical assistance.

- **Children's Support**: Ensure your children have access to counseling or support groups if they struggle with the changes in their family dynamic.

Negotiating a custody agreement with a narcissistic ex-partner requires a careful, well-prepared approach underpinned by legal advice and support. By focusing on the children's best interests, maintaining clear communication, and protecting your emotional well-being, you can navigate this challenging process more effectively, laying the groundwork for a stable and supportive environment for your children.

PROTECTING YOUR LEGAL RIGHTS WHILE MINIMIZING CONFLICT

Asserting one's legal rights in the face of a narcissistic ex does not inevitably lead to an escalation of conflict. It is entirely feasible to stand firm on your legal grounds, advocating for your and your children's well-being while simultaneously adopting strategies to reduce unnecessary confrontations. This delicate balance demands a nuanced and detailed approach, blending assertiveness with a strategic, peace-focused mindset.

Understanding Your Legal Standing

The first step in this process is to understand your legal rights and children's rights within the framework of family law. This knowledge acts as both a shield and compass, guiding your actions and decisions while protecting your family unit from potential legal overreach by a narcissistic ex-partner.

- **Consult with a Family Law Specialist**: Engage the services of a lawyer specializing in family law. Their expertise can shed light on the specifics of your legal standing and advise on the best course of action in various scenarios.

- **Educate Yourself on Local Laws**: Every jurisdiction has its nuances in family law. Take the initiative to educate yourself on the statutes and precedents relevant to your situation. This proactive step can empower you to make informed decisions.

Strategic Communication

In interactions with your narcissistic ex-partner, especially those about legal matters, how you communicate can significantly impact the potential for conflict. Strive for communication that is direct, devoid of ambiguity, yet devoid of provocation.

- **Use Written Communication**: Whenever possible, opt for email or text messages when communicating about legal matters. This approach provides a clear record of what was said, reducing the potential for misinterpretation or manipulation.

- **Choose Your Words Carefully**: Focus on stating facts and avoid language perceived as accusatory. This strategic approach can help keep exchanges civil and focused on the matter.

Setting Boundaries

Clear boundaries are crucial in managing interactions with a narcissistic ex, particularly regarding legal issues. These boundaries help delineate what is acceptable and what is not, providing a clear guideline for both parties' behaviors and expectations.

- **Be Explicit About Boundaries**: Clearly articulate your boundaries, especially those that pertain to legal interactions and co-parenting arrangements. Having these boundaries in writing can serve as a reference point for both parties.

- **Enforce Boundaries Consistently**: Once set, enforcing these boundaries is vital. If a boundary is crossed, refer to your agreed-upon terms and communicate the need to adhere to them. You must document and report each violation. If the narcissist is allowed to get away with an infraction once, it will encourage them to do it again. As onerous as it may be, you need to document each violation and pursue the consequences.

Leveraging Mediation and Legal Counsel

In scenarios where direct negotiation with a narcissistic ex becomes untenable, mediation and legal counsel offer alternative pathways for resolving disputes without escalating conflict.

- **Mediation as a First Resort**: Before pursuing court action, consider mediation. A neutral third party can facilitate discussions, helping to find mutually agreeable solutions. Mediation often proves less adversarial, reducing the potential for conflict.

- **Legal Representation in Negotiations**: Having a lawyer represent you in negotiations can remove the personal element from legal discussions, making it easier to stay focused on the issues without emotional entanglement.

Focusing on the Well-Being of Children

In all legal matters, the well-being of your children should remain the central focus. By keeping discussions and legal actions centered on what is best for the children, you might be able to find common ground with a narcissistic ex or at least minimize the areas of conflict.

- **Highlight the Children's Needs**: In communications and negotiations, consistently focus on the children's needs and well-being. This approach can help to depersonalize the conflict and find solutions that serve the children's best interests.

Utilizing Support Systems

Navigating legal disputes and asserting your rights against a narcissistic ex can be draining, both emotionally and mentally. Leaning on your support system can provide the strength and perspective needed to navigate these challenges effectively.

- **Seek Emotional Support**: Contact friends, family, or support groups who understand your situation. Their support can offer the emotional resilience needed to stand firm in your legal rights.

- **Professional Guidance**: Beyond legal counsel, consider seeking the support of a therapist or counselor. They can offer strategies to manage stress and maintain your mental health throughout the legal process.

In asserting your legal rights while striving to minimize conflict with a narcissistic ex-partner, a strategic, informed, and balanced approach is paramount. By understanding your legal standing, communicating strategically, setting clear boundaries, and focusing on the children's well-being, you can navigate the legal aspects of co-parenting to protect your rights and foster a more peaceful co-parenting environment. By leveraging mediation, legal counsel, and your support systems, you equip yourself with the tools to face legal challenges confidently while focusing on creating the best possible outcomes for your children.

FINANCIAL SURVIVAL CHECKLIST FOR CO-PARENTING WITH A NARCISSISTIC EX

Addressing financial matters while co-parenting with a narcissist requires a thoughtful and proactive approach. A financial survival checklist is a solid and concrete tool you should consider using to handle potential problems proactively.

First and foremost, establishing a solid budget is critical. This budget should account for both expected and unexpected child-related expenses. Start by listing all monthly income sources, followed by regular expenses. Remember to include savings for future needs and potential emergencies. This foundational step creates a clear financial picture, enabling you to make informed decisions and adjustments as necessary.

Creating separate financial entities is another vital aspect. If you haven't already, open bank accounts and credit lines solely in your name. This separation is crucial for establishing financial independence and protecting your assets from any form of manipulation or control attempts by the narcissistic ex-partner.

Moreover, securing legal agreements regarding financial responsibilities is non-negotiable. Whether child support, shared educational expenses, summer camps, activities, or healthcare costs, having these agreements in writing and legally recognized provides a safety net, ensuring that financial obligations are met and disputes can be resolved more efficiently. You must do this.

Maintaining meticulous records of all financial transactions related to co-parenting is also essential. This includes keeping receipts, logging child support payments received or made, and tracking all out-of-pocket expenses. Should disputes arise, this documentation is undeniable proof of compliance and responsibility. Again, consider getting a co-parenting app to assist with all of this.

To further safeguard your financial stability, explore avenues for enhancing your income. This might involve seeking career advancement opportunities, considering side ventures, or investing in personal development to increase earning potential. Diversifying your income sources contributes to financial resilience and offers peace of mind.

In addition to these strategic measures, it's essential to cultivate a support network. This network can include financial advisors, legal counsel, and peer support groups. These resources can offer valuable advice, emotional support, and practical assistance, helping you navigate the complexities of co-parenting with a narcissist.

This financial survival checklist lays the groundwork for a stable, secure co-parenting arrangement. It's a path marked by informed decisions, proactive planning, and an unwavering focus on the well-being of your children. As you move forward, remember that financial independence is not just about numbers in a bank account—it's about freedom, empowerment, and the ability to provide a nurturing environment for your children, free from the constraints of a narcissistic ex-partner.

In closing, remember the power of preparation, the importance of independence, and the value of education. These principles not only guide you through the financial aspects of co-parenting with a narcissist but also enrich your journey toward a fulfilling and resilient life. As we transition to the next chapter, let's carry forward the lessons learned, applying them with wisdom and courage as we navigate the road ahead.

Chapter 5

Understanding Parallel Parenting

Imagine standing at a crossroads where each path represents a different approach to co-parenting after a divorce with a narcissistic ex. One path is well-trodden, marked by attempts at cooperative co-parenting, fraught with conflict and stress. The other less visible and often misunderstood path leads to parallel parenting—a less conventional yet increasingly recognized route that promises a smoother ride for both parents and children. This chapter explains parallel parenting, dissecting its fundamentals and showcasing how it can serve as a viable, conflict-minimizing strategy for raising children post-divorce.

THE FUNDAMENTALS OF PARALLEL PARENTING

There are times when, despite best efforts, traditional methods of cooperative co-parenting with a narcissist do not work. It is disheartening and overwhelming, but there is another option: Parallel Parenting. Parallel parenting is most effective in high-conflict situations where nothing else seems to work. It's a structured approach that significantly reduces direct interaction between parents, thereby minimizing conflict. Yet, it ensures both parents remain actively involved in their children's lives. Think of it as two lanes on a highway, where each parent travels in their own lane, heading in the same direction but without encroaching on the other's space.

How Parallel Parenting Differs from Co-Parenting

While traditional co-parenting encourages open communication and collaborative decision-making, parallel parenting sets boundaries that limit communication to essential information only, often relayed through written means or third-party tools. Here, decisions about day-to-day parenting are made independently, reducing opportunities for conflict and stress. Often, when dealing with a narcissistic ex, Parallel Parenting is the only viable solution.

Why Choose Parallel Parenting?

For parents exiting relationships marked by narcissism, the usual co-parenting advice doesn't quite fit. The constant negotiation and interaction can become a battlefield, with children caught in the crossfire. Parallel parenting offers an alternative, prioritizing children's well-being by maintaining parental involvement while shielding them from parental conflicts.

Here are the Key Components of Parallel Parenting

- **Limited Direct Communication**: Communication is restricted to essential information concerning the children's welfare and is typically conducted in writing.

- **Independent Decision-Making**: Each parent makes daily decisions regarding the children during their custodial time without needing the other parent's approval.

- **Use of Third Parties**: For situations requiring discussion, third parties or legal tools facilitate communication, keeping interactions focused and professional.

In a nutshell, the main difference between co-parenting and parallel parenting is that in co-parenting, parents work together to create a common parenting vision and provide consistent expectations of routines in both homes. In contrast, in parallel parenting, each parent is free to act as they wish (within reason) regardless of expectations or routines set in the other home. To better understand the differences between Co-Parenting and Parallel parenting, here are some basic examples that should illustrate the differences between the two parenting models.

Let's say a child wants to go to a friend's house for a sleepover. A child raised by parents practicing co-parenting would have the same rule: either the child is allowed to go on sleepovers, or not the child is not allowed to go on sleepovers. This rule would be consistent regardless of which parent's house the child stayed in during the sleepover. This means that if the parents had agreed that sleepovers are not allowed, the child would not be allowed to go, regardless of which parent they were staying with at the time of the sleepover. Using the same example of the child wanting to go on a sleepover at a friend's house, if the child was being raised by parents practicing parallel parenting, then the decision as to whether or not the child could go on the sleepover would be completely up to the parent who was with the child at the time of the sleepover. This means if Parent A said yes, sleepovers are allowed and Parent B said no, sleepovers are not allowed, then the child would be allowed to go if they were staying at Parent A's house, and the child would not be allowed to go if they were staying at the house of Parent B. Let's take another example to help illustrate the differences between the two parenting styles. This time, we will use the example of attending religious services. In co-parenting, both parents would agree either that the kids will attend weekly religious services regardless of which parent's house they are at or that no, the kids will not attend weekly religious services regardless of which parent's house they are at. Using this same example, in parallel parenting the child might attend religious services every week when staying with parent and not attend weekly religious services when staying with Parent B. In co-parenting, the parents agree upon and have input into the child's activities, which is constant regardless of which house the child stays at. In parallel parenting, the activities are solely up to the parent with whom the child stays. Here is another way that co-parenting differs from parallel parenting: let's look at how routine events like parent/teacher conferences work. In the case of co-parenting, both parents would attend the parent/teacher conference together simultaneously. In the case of parallel parenting, the parents would request two separate parent/teacher conferences. If the school allows one parent-teacher conference, then one parent would attend the conference, and the other parent would receive an email from the school informing them about the meeting.

Setting the Stage for Parallel Parenting

The transition to parallel parenting starts with an explicit, legally binding agreement outlining each parent's rights and responsibilities. This plan covers major decisions like education, healthcare, and religious upbringing, alongside a detailed parenting schedule. The agreement should be as specific as possible, detailing pick-up and drop-off arrangements, holiday schedules, and procedures for making alterations to the plan.

Communication Protocols

Establishing a communication protocol is crucial. This usually involves using a dedicated co-parenting app that keeps records of all exchanges. These protocols serve as a buffer, reducing the emotional charge of direct communication and maintaining focus on the children's needs.

Boundaries and Self-Care

Setting and respecting boundaries is essential for the parallel parenting arrangement. This extends to self-care practices for managing stress and emotional well-being. Remember, the ultimate goal is to create a peaceful and stable environment for the children, free from the turmoil of parental conflicts.

Parallel parenting isn't about disengaging from your role as a parent. It's about redefining how you navigate that role in a high-conflict co-parenting situation. By minimizing direct interactions and focusing on structured, independent parenting, this approach offers peace and stability for both parents and children. As we continue to explore parallel parenting, remember that the essence of this strategy lies in its ability to provide children with the love and support of both parents without the shadow of conflict darkening their experiences.

SETTING UP A PARALLEL PARENTING PLAN: ESSENTIAL COMPONENTS

Crafting a parallel parenting plan requires attention to detail and focusing on the needs and welfare of the children involved. This plan acts as a map, guiding both parents in navigating their responsibilities while minimizing direct contact to reduce potential conflicts. A well-thought-out plan is not just a document but an agreement, usually recorded in the court, that adapts to the changing needs of children as they grow.

Identifying Key Areas of Responsibility

The first step in developing a parallel parenting plan involves outlining the main areas of responsibility that need clear delineation. These include but are not limited to:

- **Healthcare**: Decisions regarding the children's health, including choice of healthcare providers, emergency care procedures, and routine check-ups.

- **Education**: Choices about schooling, including the selection of educational institutions, participation in extracurricular activities, and attending parent-teacher conferences.

- **Living Arrangements**: Clarity on primary residence visitation schedules, including holidays, birthdays, and vacation periods, ensuring children have predictable routines.

- **Financial Obligations**: An explicit agreement on financial responsibilities covering child support, educational costs, healthcare expenses, and extracurricular activities.

For each area, the plan should define who has decision-making authority and how information will be shared between parents.

Developing a Communication Strategy

Given the goal of minimizing direct contact, establishing an effective communication strategy is vital. The plan should specify:

- **Preferred Communication Channels**: Designate specific platforms for exchanging information about children's well-being, such as a specialized co-parenting app.

- **Frequency of Updates**: Agree on a regular schedule for updates on the children's well-being, academic progress, and health status to ensure both parents are informed. This update should be communicated through the app or a third party, such as a GAL or a lawyer.

- **Emergency Communication Protocol**: Outline a straightforward procedure for emergencies, ensuring that both parents understand how to convey urgent information swiftly and efficiently.

This structured approach to communication ensures that necessary information is shared without unnecessary interaction, reducing the potential for conflict.

Scheduling Considerations

A detailed schedule is a cornerstone of any parallel parenting plan. This schedule should be comprehensive, covering:

- **Routine Visitation**: Delineate the regular visitation schedule, including weekdays and weekends, and considerations for travel time and logistics.

- **Special Occasions**: Specify arrangements for holidays, birthdays, and special events, rotating them between parents as agreed to ensure fairness.

- **Vacations**: Include guidelines for vacation times, notice periods for planning, and sharing of vacation schedules.

A well-defined schedule offers predictability and stability for children, providing them a sense of security amidst their parents' separate lives.

Handling Adjustments and Disputes

Despite the best planning, adjustments to the parenting plan may be necessary as children grow and circumstances change. The plan should, therefore, include:

- **Process for Making Adjustments**: Outline a procedure for proposing, discussing, and agreeing on adjustments to the parenting plan, possibly involving mediation to resolve disagreements.

- **Dispute Resolution Mechanism**: Define a straightforward process for resolving disputes, prioritizing mediation or arbitration over litigation to maintain a focus on the children's best interests.

By anticipating the need for adjustments and providing mechanisms for dispute resolution, the plan remains flexible and adaptable to the family's evolving needs.

Regular Review and Revision

Finally, the dynamic nature of family life necessitates regular reviews of the parallel parenting plan. This can be scheduled annually or bi-annually, allowing both parents to reflect on what is working, what needs adjustment, and how the plan can better serve the changing needs of the children. These reviews should be approached with an open mind and a commitment to co-parenting positively despite the challenges.

In constructing a parallel parenting plan, the goal is to create a framework that minimizes conflict, supports the children's developmental needs, and respects the autonomy of each parent. By focusing on clear communication, detailed scheduling, and provisions for flexibility and parental well-being, the plan lays the groundwork for a healthier post-divorce family dynamic.

COMMUNICATING THROUGH THIRD PARTIES AND LEGAL TOOLS

Navigating co-parenting with a narcissistic ex often presents a unique set of challenges, especially when it comes to communication. High-conflict situations can significantly benefit from the involvement of third parties or the use of specialized legal tools designed to streamline communication, thereby reducing stress and potential conflicts. This approach allows parents to focus on their children's needs without getting embroiled in personal disputes that can detract from effective parenting.

Advantages of Third-Party Mediation

In scenarios where direct communication becomes a battlefield, enlisting the help of a professional mediator can provide a neutral ground for discussion. Mediators are trained to facilitate conversations, ensuring that both parties' perspectives are heard and respected. **This structured setting can help reach agreements on contentious issues by:**

- Providing an unbiased perspective that can help clarify misunderstandings and bring objectivity to emotionally charged discussions.

- Offering creative solutions the parents might not have considered opens new avenues for agreement.

- Encouraging a focus on the well-being of the children, which can sometimes get lost in direct exchanges between parents.

Parents might find that using a mediator for developing or revising their parenting plan can lead to more durable and mutually satisfactory outcomes.

Leveraging Co-parenting Coordinators

Engaging a co-parenting coordinator can be invaluable for managing high-conflict co-parenting situations. These professionals act as a buffer between parents, handling communication regarding scheduling, transitions, and daily co-parenting decisions. Their involvement can significantly reduce direct contact, which can be particularly beneficial in minimizing opportunities for conflict. Co-parenting coordinators can assist by:

- Monitoring adherence to the parenting plan and helping resolve disputes regarding interpreting or implementing its terms.

- Facilitating communication about changes in scheduling or addressing unforeseen issues that require cooperation.

- When needed, provide recommendations for counseling or support services to support the family's adjustment to the co-parenting arrangement.

Utilizing Legal Tools for Communication

In addition to third-party intermediaries, several co-parenting apps have been developed to aid in co-parenting communication. One app that particularly seems to work well for parallel parenting is being approved for use in most courts is our family wizard, but be sure to do your own research and select the best tools and apps for our specific situation. These tools are designed to minimize conflict by structuring the exchange of information in a clear, trackable way and less susceptible to manipulation. Benefits include:

- **Documented Exchanges**: All communication is logged and can be easily accessed for reference, reducing disputes about who said what and when.

- **Controlled Interaction**: By limiting the types of communication on these platforms, parents are encouraged to keep exchanges focused on the children's needs.

- **Accessibility**: Information about the children's schedules, medical records, school reports, and other important documents can be shared in one accessible location, ensuring both parents have the information they need to make informed decisions.

Platforms such as these can offer security and fairness, as both parents have equal access to information and an equal opportunity to contribute to their children's lives.

Guidelines for Effective Use of Third Parties and Legal Tools

To maximize the benefits of involving third parties or utilizing legal tools, consider the following guidelines:

- **Clear Objectives**: Before engaging a mediator or co-parenting coordinator, define clear objectives for what you hope to achieve. This preparation ensures that sessions are focused and productive.

- **Choose Wisely**: Take the time to select professionals or platforms well-suited to your family's specific needs. Look for individuals with experience in high-conflict co-parenting situations and platforms that offer the features most relevant to your communication challenges.

- **Commit to the Process**: For third-party mediation or coordination to be effective, parents must be willing to participate in good faith. This includes being open to the suggestions of the mediator or coordinator and adhering to the agreed-upon communication protocols.

- **Maintain Respect**: Respect for the other parent is crucial, even in structured settings. This includes respecting their time by being punctual for meetings and their perspective by listening without interruption or judgment.

Incorporating these approaches into your co-parenting strategy can create a more structured, less stressful communication environment. This benefits you and your ex-partner and, most importantly, creates a more peaceful and stable atmosphere for your children.

ESTABLISHING FIRM BOUNDARIES IN PARALLEL PARENTING

In parallel parenting, establishing clear and firm boundaries is non-negotiable, ensuring each parent can maintain independence while minimizing the chance for disputes. These boundaries provide a framework that guides each parent through the complexities of raising children post-separation. They are agreements rooted in mutual respect and the goal of fostering a nurturing environment for the children involved.

The Importance of Clearly Defined Boundaries

Boundaries in parallel parenting do more than delineate what is acceptable; they safeguard each parent's autonomy, creating a buffer that reduces interaction and, by extension, potential conflict. This clarity is crucial in interactions with a narcissistic ex-partner, where misunderstandings can quickly escalate.

Boundaries act as a pre-agreed-upon set of rules, a common language both parents commit to following for their children's well-being.

- **Personal Space and Time**: Respecting each parent's time with the children, without interference, ensures that both parents can fully engage in their parenting time, free from unsolicited input or criticism.

- **Communication Guidelines**: Setting clear expectations for how and when communication will occur, specifying the topics that are open for discussion, and agreeing on the preferred method of communication, be it through a co-parenting app or email, helps prevent miscommunications.

- **Decision Making**: Clearly outlining who makes daily decisions and who is responsible for larger, life-impacting decisions prevents overlap and reduces the chances for disagreement. It's about agreeing on who can decide what, ensuring that both parents still play active roles in their children's lives.

Steps to Establishing Boundaries

Setting these boundaries begins with an open dialogue, where both parties come together to discuss their needs and expectations. This might initially seem daunting, especially in high-conflict relationships, but it is a necessary step toward creating a stable parallel parenting arrangement.

- **Identify Key Areas**: Start by identifying the areas where boundaries are needed. This includes, but is not limited to, communication, parenting time, financial responsibilities, and decision-making processes.

- **Draft a Written Agreement**: Once these areas are identified, draft a written agreement that outlines the boundaries in clear, unambiguous language. This document should then be reviewed and, if necessary, refined through negotiation until both parties find it acceptable.

- **Legal Review and Approval**: For added security and enforceability, have the agreement reviewed by legal professionals and, if possible, incorporated into the official custody arrangement. This legal backing ensures that the boundaries weigh mutual agreement, providing a means for recourse should one party consistently fail to respect them.

Navigating Boundary Violations

Even with the best-laid plans, boundary violations can occur. How these violations are handled can significantly impact the effectiveness of the parallel parenting arrangement.

- **Immediate Address**: When a boundary is crossed, address the issue promptly. Delaying or ignoring the violation only undermines the agreement and can lead to further encroachments.

- **Stick to the Facts**: When discussing the violation, focus on the facts and the specific terms of the agreement that were not upheld. Avoid accusatory language or emotional responses, which can escalate the situation.

- **Seek Mediation if Necessary**: If violations persist or there is a dispute about the interpretation of the boundaries, seeking mediation can provide a neutral ground for resolving the issue. Mediators can help clarify misunderstandings and facilitate a return to compliance with the established boundaries.

In parallel parenting, setting and respecting firm boundaries is not about creating distance but defining a new way to co-parent that minimizes conflict and maximizes each parent's ability to contribute positively to their children's lives. It's a structured approach that acknowledges the challenges while focusing on the most important outcome: the well-being and happiness of the children. Through clear boundaries, open communication, and a commitment to flexibility and respect, parents can navigate the complexities of raising children separately but equally, ensuring a stable and nurturing environment for their most cherished ones.

SUCCESS STORIES: THRIVING IN A PARALLEL PARENTING ARRANGEMENT

The real-world application of parallel parenting, with the added complexity of a narcissistic ex-partner, has repeatedly demonstrated its efficacy, with numerous families moving to healthier dynamics and happier children. These stories serve as proof of concept and hope for those finding themselves at the beginning of their parallel parenting paths. Let's explore how diverse families have found peace and positivity through this approach.

A Tale of Two Cities

In one notable instance, a family divided between two cities found solace in the structure parallel parenting provided. Initially, the distance was a source of contention, with disagreements over travel arrangements and visitation schedules. However, after adopting a parallel parenting model, both parents could establish routines in their respective cities that worked for them and their children. Key to their success was using a shared online calendar for scheduling visits and a mutually agreed-upon communication app for discussing the children's needs. A case that underscores the importance of balancing parental involvement involved parents who lived in different cities. The distance created challenges in maintaining consistent parental involvement. Their solution was to design a co-parenting plan that maximized the quality of time both parents spent with the children despite the physical distance. Some of the ways they were able to accomplish this are as follows.

- **Creative Scheduling**: They crafted a schedule allowing extended stays with each parent during school breaks, ensuring that both parents remained actively involved in the children's lives.

- **Virtual Interaction**: They also incorporated regular video calls and virtual activities into their plan, allowing the children to feel connected to the non-residential parent even when apart.

- **Outcome**: This thoughtful approach to scheduling and communication helped maintain strong bonds between the children and both parents.

From Conflict to Cooperation

Another success story comes from a family that struggled with relentless conflict after their separation. Tensions ran high, and communication often devolved into arguments, impacting the emotional well-being of their children. The turning point came when both parents agreed to engage a family mediator who helped them transition to a parallel parenting arrangement. By limiting direct contact and focusing on written communication through a so-parenting app for essential discussions about the children, they significantly reduced the contentious nature of their interactions. The children benefited from a more stable and peaceful home environment, free from the stress of parental conflicts.

The Power of Boundaries

A further instance of parallel parenting success was seen in a family where setting firm boundaries transformed the co-parenting relationship. Initially, one parent frequently overstepped, making unilateral decisions about the children's activities and schooling without consulting the other. Introducing a detailed parallel parenting plan with clear guidelines on decision-making authority and communication protocols helped establish much-needed boundaries. This structure allowed both parents to feel respected and empowered, leading to a more harmonious dynamic that placed the children's interests at the forefront.

These stories, each unique in their context and challenges, share a common thread of positive transformation through the adoption of parallel parenting. They illustrate that even in situations marked by distance, conflict, or imbalance in parental involvement, it is possible to create a co-parenting arrangement that nurtures the children's well-being and supports the parents' ability to move forward positively.

In reflecting on these narratives, it becomes clear that parallel parenting is the best solution for parents who cannot get along and are in a continual state of high conflict. This approach's structure, boundaries, and independence ensure reduced conflict, enhanced cooperation, and, most importantly, happier and healthier children.

Another important benefit of parallel parenting is the parents' enhanced well-being. By removing the interaction between the narcissistic parent and the counter-parent, the stress level of each parent immediately decreases. As we conclude this exploration of parallel parenting, we are reminded of the resilience of families and the adaptability of parenting strategies to meet the needs of children and parents alike. These success stories demonstrate the effectiveness of parallel parenting and act as encouragement for those considering this approach as they raise their children.

Next, we look to nurturing resilience in ourselves and our children, reinforcing that out of adversity comes strength, growth, and a deeper understanding of what it means to parent effectively, even in the most challenging circumstances.

I hope you are enjoying this book. I would love to hear your thoughts on this book.

Many readers are unaware of how difficult it is to get reviews and how much they help authors like me.

I would greatly appreciate it if you could support me and help get the word out to others about this book.

To leave a review, please either click on/ or use the link below or scan the QR code with your phone. I am very grateful for your support.

https://www.amazon.com/review/create-review/?ie=UTF8&channel=glance-detail&asin=B0CTHPKQDB

Chapter 6

The Importance of Boundaries

Boundaries are one of the most important things to establish and enforce when dealing with a Narcissist. If your ex is a narcissist and you are raising children with them, this won't be very easy. You must learn how to do this for both you and your children.

STEP-BY-STEP GUIDE TO ESTABLISHING BOUNDARIES

Identify Your Needs and Limits

Start by taking stock of what you need to feel secure and respected in your co-parenting arrangement. Whether you are high-conflict co-parenting or parallel parenting, if you are doing this with a narcissist, you need to think this through. Consider your non-negotiables, like no communication past a certain hour or the necessity of written agreements for changes in scheduling. It's about clarifying your needs to maintain your well-being and effectively parent your children.

- **Reflect on past interactions**: Think about moments that left you feeling stressed or disrespected. These instances often highlight areas where boundaries are needed.

- **Consider your children's needs**: Reflect on what arrangements best support your children's emotional and physical well-being. Their needs should be at the forefront of any boundary-setting process.

Communicate Your Boundaries Clearly.

Once you've identified your boundaries, the next step is to communicate them to your ex-partner. Narcissists do not think boundaries apply to themselves, so steady yourself and be prepared for the drama that will undoubtedly be unleashed upon you by your narcissistic ex. Deliver the message, stay calm and detached, and do not react. Approach it with a focus on the well-being of your children and the desire to create a cooperative co-parenting environment.

- **Choose a neutral setting**: Have this conversation in a neutral setting where both of you feel at ease.

- **Use "I" statements**: Frame your boundaries in terms of your own needs and feelings to avoid placing blame or starting a conflict. For example, "I feel overwhelmed when discussions go late into the night. I need all our calls to happen before 8 PM."

Implement Boundaries with Consistency

For boundaries to be effective, they must be consistently upheld. This might require you to remind your ex-partner of the agreed-upon limits occasionally.

- **Stay firm but respectful**: If a boundary is crossed, address it promptly and calmly, reiterating the need for the boundary and its importance for the co-parenting relationship.

- **Be ready to adapt**: Life changes, and so might your boundaries. Be open to revisiting and adjusting them as needed, always focusing on what's best for the children.

Setting boundaries with a narcissist can be extremely tricky. Now that you have thought and figured out your boundaries, write them down. When you meet with your ex, bring this to ensure you clearly express your exact needs regarding boundaries. If you are working with a GAL and/or a lawyer, loop them in on this conversation for support. Remember the Grey Rock Method: do not react, do not feed their supply, and do not engage in drama and hysteria. Being clear with your boundaries, including your GAL or lawyer, and using the Grey Rock Method will ensure you cover all necessary points and express your needs clearly. This should foster a productive discussion, minimizing misunderstandings and laying a solid foundation to build upon.

- **Prepare what you want to say**: List the boundaries you must establish and why they're important.

- **Anticipate responses**: Think about how your ex-partner might respond and plan how to address their concerns while still upholding your boundaries.

- **Focus on the children**: Keep the conversation centered on the children's well-being, which can help keep the discussion constructive.

Establishing boundaries in co-parenting or parallel parenting with a narcissistic ex is about creating a space where you can parent effectively and maintain your sanity. It's not about building walls to keep the other parent out but about setting clear guidelines that allow for respectful interaction and cooperation for the sake of your children. These boundaries ensure that your co-parenting arrangement can provide stability and positivity in your children's lives.

WHAT TO DO WHEN BOUNDARIES ARE VIOLATED

In the landscape of co-parenting or parallel parenting with a narcissistic ex, boundary violations can, unfortunately, emerge as a recurring theme. These transgressions, ranging from minor oversteps to significant breaches, challenge the foundation of the structured parenting arrangement you've worked hard to establish. Addressing these violations promptly and effectively is mandatory. It is necessary for the sustained health of your parenting dynamic, your mental health, and, most importantly, for the well-being of your children.

Acknowledge and Assess the Violation

Upon encountering a boundary violation, recognize the breach and evaluate its impact. It's crucial to determine whether the violation is a minor, isolated incident, or part of a larger pattern of behavior. This assessment will guide your response and help you decide whether a simple conversation can rectify the situation or if more assertive action is required. Regardless, you must call the narcissist out on the violation and clearly and calmly state that this is not acceptable. The narcissist will see anything less as weakness and a green light to go ahead and continue to violate.

- **Document the occurrence**: Keeping a record of the violation, including the date, time, and nature of the breach is necessary, especially if the behavior becomes recurrent. Documentation creates a factual basis for discussions and, if needed, legal consultations.

- **Reflect on the children's perspective**: Consider how the violation affects your children. Their emotional and physical well-being should always guide your response strategy.

Initiate a Constructive Dialogue

If the boundary violation is relatively minor or appears to be an oversight, initiating a constructive dialogue with your ex-partner might resolve the issue. This conversation should remind them of the established boundaries and express how their violation has impacted you and potentially your children.

- **Choose a neutral tone and setting**: Aim to express your concerns without assigning blame. Just state the facts in neutral language. It is best to do this in writing so you do not engage with them and can document the incident.

- **Be specific about the violation and its effects**: Clearly articulate what boundary was crossed and how it has affected the co-parenting arrangement and your children. Specificity can prevent defensiveness and focus the conversation on resolving the issue.

Employ Mediation for Recurring or Significant Violations

Mediation can serve as an effective next step in cases where violations are significant or form a recurring pattern. A mediator provides a neutral platform for both parents to discuss the boundary issues and work towards a resolution. This professional intervention can be particularly beneficial when direct communication has failed to resolve the problem.

- **Select a mediator experienced in co-parenting issues**: Choosing a mediator who understands the complexities of co-parenting, especially in high-conflict situations, can improve the chances of reaching a productive outcome.

- **Prepare for the session**: Before mediation, outline the boundary violations, their frequency, and impact. Bring all of your documentation. This preparation ensures that the session addresses the core issues at hand.

Strengthen Boundaries Through Re-negotiation

Sometimes, boundary violations signal that the original terms may need reassessment and strengthening. This doesn't indicate failure but rather an evolution of the co-parenting arrangement. Re-negotiating boundaries can clarify expectations and reinforce the structure necessary for effective parallel parenting.

- **Involve a co-parenting counselor if needed**: A professional specializing in co-parenting can offer guidance on setting realistic and enforceable boundaries.

- **Incorporate flexibility where appropriate**: While reinforcing boundaries, consider whether certain areas can offer flexibility to accommodate life's unpredictability, always with the children's best interests at heart.

Consider Legal Recourse for Persistent Violations

Persistent and egregious boundary violations may necessitate exploring legal recourse. The only way a narcissist will pay attention and stop violating the agreed-upon terms is with legal intervention. This is unfortunate, but it might be required. This step should be considered carefully, understanding the potential impact on the co-parenting relationship and, most importantly, the children.

- **Consult with a family law attorney**: An attorney can advise on the legal options available to enforce the boundaries and protect your children's welfare.

- **Prepare your documentation**: The records you've kept of boundary violations and their impacts will be invaluable in this process, providing evidence to support your case.

Prioritize Self-Care and Support

Finally, navigating boundary violations can be emotionally taxing. Prioritizing your well-being through self-care practices and leaning on your support system can provide the emotional resilience needed during these challenging times. Ensuring you are in a healthy place mentally and emotionally is crucial for effectively managing boundary violations and maintaining a stable co-parenting or parallel parenting arrangement.

- **Engage in activities that bolster your well-being**: Whether exercising, hobbies, or spending time with loved ones, find what replenishes your energy and brings you joy.

- **Seek support from those who understand**: Connecting with friends, family, or support groups who understand the nuances of co-parenting with a narcissistic ex can offer comfort and practical advice.

Unfortunately, the reality of raising children with a narcissist means it is highly likely you will be dealing with boundary violations. Yet, you can address these challenges effectively with a strategic approach that includes acknowledgment, constructive dialogue, mediation, and, when necessary, legal action. The key to keeping your sanity is disengaging and not allowing yourself to become reactive. Deliver your message: you violated the terms of our agreement by doing this on this date and at this time. And be done with it. Do not allow the narcissist to drag you into drama. Stay calm, stay strong, take the high road, and be done. Call upon friends, family, and professionals for support and reassurance. This proactive stance not only upholds the integrity of your parenting arrangement but also safeguards the emotional and physical well-being of your most precious concern—your children.

NAVIGATING HIGH-CONFLICT SITUATIONS WITH GRACE

High-conflict scenarios in co-parenting or parallel parenting arrangements, especially with a narcissistic ex-partner, are not just challenging; they test your patience and emotional resilience. Here, the focus shifts towards managing these situations not just to diffuse tension but to ensure the well-being of your children remains the priority. Handling these moments requires strategic communication, emotional intelligence, and a deep commitment to safeguarding your children's interests.

Strategies for Managing Communication

Effective communication becomes your first line of defense in high-conflict situations. It's not merely about what is said but how it's conveyed. Adopting a calm, clear, and concise approach to communication can prevent many conflicts from escalating.

- **Write it down**: Opt for written communication when possible. This gives you the time to think about your response and ensures a record of what was said.

- **Stay on topic**: Keep conversations focused solely on the issue, avoiding personal remarks or past grievances that might inflame the situation.

- **Choose neutral language**: Word choices matter. Use neutral and objective language, steering clear of words that carry an emotional or judgmental tone.

Emotional Intelligence in Action

Emotional intelligence plays a crucial role in navigating high-conflict scenarios. It involves recognizing your emotions and those of your ex-partner, managing them effectively, and responding to situations with empathy and understanding.

- **Self-awareness**: Be mindful of your emotional triggers and take steps to manage your reactions. This might mean taking a moment to breathe and compose yourself before responding.

- **Empathy**: Try to see the situation from your ex-partner's perspective, even if you disagree. Understanding their viewpoint can provide insights into how best to approach a resolution.

- **De-escalation techniques**: Use calming tactics such as agreeing to discuss the issue later or suggesting a break if conversations become too heated.

Prioritizing the Children's Perspective

In every high-conflict interaction, the impact on the children should be at the forefront of your considerations. Their emotional and physical well-being depends on how effectively you manage and minimize these conflicts.

- **Shield the children from disputes**: Avoid discussing contentious issues or expressing negative emotions about the other parent in front of the children.

- **Maintain routines**: Keep the children's daily routines as stable as possible, providing them a sense of security amidst the parental conflicts.

- **Open lines of communication**: Encourage your children to express their feelings about the situation, offering them reassurance and support.

Seeking External Support

Sometimes, external support becomes necessary to navigate through particularly challenging conflicts. This support can come in various forms, tailored to the situation's specific needs.

- **Professional counseling**: Engaging a therapist or counselor for yourself or your children can provide a safe space to work through emotions and develop coping mechanisms.

- **Legal advice**: In cases where conflicts might have legal implications, consulting with a family law attorney can offer clarity and direction on how to proceed.

- **Co-parenting mediator**: A mediator specializing in co-parenting issues can facilitate discussions between you and your ex-partner, helping to find mutually acceptable solutions.

Creating a Personal Support Network

Beyond professional support, building a personal network of friends, family, and peers who understand your situation can be invaluable. This network offers emotional support, practical advice, and a much-needed sense of community.

- **Join support groups**: Connect with others in similar situations through local or online support groups. Sharing experiences and strategies can be incredibly empowering.

- **Lean on loved ones**: Don't hesitate to contact close friends or family when you need to talk or seek advice. They can offer a listening ear and a different perspective on the situation.

Self-Care as a Priority

While managing high-conflict scenarios, self-care often takes a back seat. However, nurturing your physical and emotional health is crucial for maintaining the strength and clarity to handle these challenges effectively.

- **Establish a self-care routine**: Incorporate activities into your daily routine that reduce stress and promote well-being, such as exercise, meditation, or hobbies.

- **Set aside time for relaxation**: Ensure you have downtime to decompress and recharge, whether reading a book, walking, or enjoying a favorite show.

Navigating high-conflict situations with grace is not about avoiding confrontation at all costs but about choosing your battles wisely, communicating effectively, and always keeping the well-being of your children in focus. You can manage these conflicts by employing strategies that promote clear communication, emotional intelligence, and a strong support network to protect your peace and provide your children with a stable, nurturing environment.

ENFORCING BOUNDARIES THROUGH LEGAL MEANS

In co-parenting or parallel parenting with a narcissistic ex, there are times when setting and communicating boundaries might not be enough. Despite clear agreements and earnest attempts at dialogue, some ex-partners might persist in violating, disregarding the established limits crucial for maintaining a peaceful and constructive parenting relationship. In these instances, turning to legal avenues to enforce boundaries becomes necessary—a step taken to safeguard your well-being and, most importantly, that of your children.

The Decision to Pursue Legal Intervention

The choice to involve legal mechanisms is significant and often arrives after much consideration. It marks a point where other methods to uphold boundaries have been tried and found wanting, where the frequency or severity of boundary violations impact the children's emotional or physical well-being. It's a recognition that external authority is required to bring about compliance and respect for agreed-upon limits.

- **Document Patterns of Violation**: Before moving forward, ensure that there is a clear record of instances where boundaries were disregarded. This documentation should include dates, descriptions, and, if applicable, any communication between you and your ex-partner regarding the violation.

- **Seek Legal Counsel**: Engage with a legal professional specializing in family law, ideally with experience in high-conflict co-parenting situations. They can guide you on the most appropriate legal actions tailored to your circumstances.

Legal Tools and Approaches

Several legal avenues can be pursued to enforce boundaries, each with its own processes and potential outcomes. The choice of which path to follow should be made in consultation with your legal advisor, considering what is most likely to bring about the desired respect for boundaries while prioritizing the children's best interests.

- **Modification of Custody Orders**: If boundary violations directly impact the children's well-being, petitioning the court to modify existing custody orders might be warranted. This could include adjustments to visitation schedules or decision-making authorities to protect the children better.

- **Restraining Orders**: In situations where violations escalate to harassment or pose a threat to safety, obtaining a restraining order against the ex-partner might be necessary. Such orders are serious legal instruments designed to prevent further harm.

- **Contempt Proceedings**: If an ex-partner is found to violate a legally binding agreement or court order, filing for contempt proceedings can compel compliance. These proceedings can result in various penalties designed to enforce adherence to the court's directives.

Preparing for Legal Proceedings

The road to enforcing boundaries through legal means demands preparation and clarity. It involves a thorough understanding of the legal process and readiness to articulate how the violations affect the children and the co-parenting dynamic.

- **Gather Evidence**: Compile all relevant documentation, including communication records, a log of violations, and any evidence of the impact these actions have had on the children.

- **Witness Statements**: If others have witnessed boundary violations or their effects, their statements can add weight to your case. This might include teachers, counselors, or family members who have observed changes in the children's behavior or well-being.

- **Legal Representation**: Ensure that you have competent legal representation, a professional who can navigate the complexities of family law, and understands your situation's nuances. They will be your advocate, presenting your case clearly and effectively to achieve the best possible outcome.

The Impact on Children

The children's welfare is at the heart of the decision to enforce boundaries legally. Every legal action should be weighed against its potential impact on them, with their emotional and physical well-being as the guiding principle.

- **Minimize Exposure**: Shield the children from legal proceedings as much as possible. While older children might be aware of the situation, reassuring them of their safety and stability is crucial. Children mustn't feel responsible for their parent's actions.

- **Professional Support**: Consider enlisting the help of child psychologists or counselors to help the children navigate any feelings of uncertainty or stress related to the legal actions being taken.

Turning to legal measures to enforce co-parenting boundaries is a step taken carefully, rooted in the desire to create a respectful, stable environment for your children to thrive. It is often necessary when dealing with a narcissistic ex. It underscores a commitment to uphold the structures needed for their well-being, even in the face of challenges that require judicial intervention.

TEACHING CHILDREN THE IMPORTANCE OF BOUNDARIES

In family dynamics, especially in consideration of co-parenting or parallel parenting with a narcissistic ex, imparting the value of boundaries to children is a pivotal aspect of their emotional and relational development. This education gives them the skills to navigate the complexities of dual households and lays the groundwork for future interactions and relationships.

The essence of teaching children about boundaries revolves around helping them understand their own space, emotions, and needs and how to respectfully communicate and assert these aspects in their interactions with both parents. It's about instilling a sense of respect and empathy, ensuring they grow into individuals capable of forming healthy, balanced relationships.

Initiating Conversations About Boundaries

Initiating open discussions about the concept of boundaries is the first step. These conversations should be age-appropriate and grounded in examples relevant to their daily experiences. For younger children, this might involve simple explanations about personal space or the importance of asking before taking a sibling's toy. For older children and teenagers, the dialogue can expand to include discussions about emotional boundaries, privacy, and the nuances of consent in various contexts.

- **Use relatable scenarios**: Draw on examples from children's books, movies, or personal experiences to illustrate boundaries and why they matter.

- **Encourage questions**: Make these conversations interactive, allowing your children to ask questions and express their thoughts about boundaries.

Modeling Boundary Setting and Respect

Children learn a great deal from observing the adults in their lives. Thus, modeling healthy boundary setting and respect in your interactions with them and others is crucial. This involves:

- **Demonstrating consent**: Always ask for permission before engaging in physical affection and respect their response, showing their autonomy is valued.

- **Respecting their boundaries**: Honor the boundaries your children set, whether it's a request for alone time or not wanting to discuss a certain topic, reinforcing the importance of mutual respect.

Practical Boundary-Setting Exercises

Engage your children in practical exercises that allow them to practice setting and respecting boundaries. Role-playing scenarios, where they can navigate hypothetical situations involving boundary setting, can be particularly effective. Additionally, creating family rules together that include boundaries around personal space, shared belongings, and family time can offer practical applications of these concepts.

- **Role-playing games**: Use imaginary scenarios or past experiences where they need to assert a boundary and guide them on handling it respectfully and effectively.

- **Family rules brainstorming**: Collaborate on a set of family rules that respect everyone's personal space, belongings, and need for privacy, highlighting how boundaries operate within the family unit.

Supporting Them in Boundary Disputes

Children will inevitably face situations where their boundaries are challenged by peers, family members, or their interactions with each parent. Providing support and guidance on how to handle these instances is key. This involves:

- **Listening without judgment**: When your child expresses a concern about a boundary being crossed, listen attentively, offering support and understanding.

- **Problem-solving together**: Discuss potential solutions or ways to assert their boundaries in the future, empowering them to handle similar situations independently.

The Role of Consistency

Consistency in discussing, respecting, and enforcing boundaries within the family environment is vital. This consistency reinforces the importance and validity of boundaries, helping children internalize these concepts as they grow. Ensure that the rules and expectations around boundaries are upheld in both households, providing a stable framework that supports their development.

By implementing boundaries into your children's upbringing, you give them the tools to manage the complexities of a dual household and the broader spectrum of relationships they will encounter throughout their lives. This education fosters a sense of respect, empathy, and self-awareness, laying a solid foundation for their emotional and relational well-being.

As this chapter draws to a close, the importance of boundaries and their role in supporting the delicate balance of co-parenting or parallel parenting with a narcissistic ex is clear. Healthy boundaries will also lead to respectful relationships in all areas of their lives. With a solid groundwork of boundary setting and respect, we focus on nurturing resilience and growth within our family dynamic, exploring further avenues to strengthen and support our children's emotional and psychological well-being.

Chapter 7

A Blueprint for Success: The Co-Parenting Plan

C reating a co-parenting plan will provide structure and clarity to what often feels impossible. You can transform chaos into harmony by laying down a framework detailing every aspect of parenting, from daily routines to decision-making processes.

COMPONENTS OF A SUCCESSFUL CO-PARENTING PLAN

The strength of an effective co-parenting plan is that it is exhaustive and has anticipated and made provisions for all foreseeable contingencies. It should leave no room for ambiguity. Here's how to ensure your co-parenting plan covers all bases:

A Clear Schedule

- **Routine Days**: Detail who the children will be with on weekdays and weekends. Consider logistics like school drop-offs and extracurricular activities, aiming for minimal disruption to the children's daily lives.

- **Holidays and Special Occasions**: Divide holidays, birthdays, and vacations, ensuring both parents have meaningful time with the children. Alternating major holidays each year can keep arrangements fair.

- **Unexpected Changes**: Include a protocol for handling last-minute changes, setting a timeframe for notifications, and an agreement on how these alterations are managed.

Decision-Making Process

- **Healthcare**: Specify who makes decisions about the children's health matters, from choosing healthcare providers to managing emergencies.

- **Education**: Outline how educational decisions are made, including the choice of schools, participation in extracurricular activities, and attendance at parent-teacher conferences.

- **General Welfare**: Determine how decisions about the children's general welfare are made, covering areas like religion, cultural upbringing, and discipline strategies.

Communication Guidelines

- **Frequency and Method**: Agree on how often and through what channels (e.g., email, co-parenting apps) you will communicate about the children.

- **Emergency Contacts**: Provide a list of emergency contacts, ensuring both parents can access essential information.

- **Respectful Tone**: Commit to maintaining a respectful tone in all communications, focusing on the children's needs.

Financial Responsibilities

- **Child Support**: Detail the child support arrangements, including payment schedules and conditions for reevaluation.

- **Additional Expenses**: Agree on how other child-related expenses (medical bills, school fees, extracurricular activities) are divided.

Parental Responsibilities and Rights

- **Access to Information**: Ensure both parents have equal access to the children's academic records, medical information, and updates on extracurricular activities.

- **Right to Privacy**: Respect each other's privacy by agreeing not to engage in behaviors like unannounced visits or using the children to gather information about the other parent.

CUSTOMIZING YOUR CO-PARENTING PLAN FOR A NARCISSISTIC EX

Crafting a co-parenting plan with a narcissistic ex requires a nuanced approach. The unpredictable nature of this relationship demands strategies that anticipate potential challenges while remaining flexible enough to adapt to unforeseen changes. Here, the focus shifts toward creating a co-parenting blueprint that addresses the standard logistical and emotional considerations and incorporates safeguards and communication mechanisms to reduce conflict and enhance cooperation.

Understanding Narcissism in the Co-Parenting Context

Recognizing how narcissistic traits manifest in co-parenting scenarios is critical. This awareness informs the customization of the co-parenting plan, ensuring it accounts for situations where the narcissistic ex's behavior might disrupt harmony and stability. For instance, narcissists often seek control and may use communication about the children to exert this control or engage in manipulation. A tailored co-parenting plan, therefore, includes specific communication protocols to minimize these opportunities, using neutral, third-party apps or software for information sharing and scheduling.

Tailored Communication Protocols

The heart of any co-parenting plan lies in its communication strategies. When dealing with a narcissistic ex, these strategies need to be particularly robust, incorporating:

- **Dedicated Channels**: Specify using a co-parenting app that logs conversations and exchanges, ensuring that all communication is transparent and accountable.

- **Content Limits**: Clearly define what types of communication are acceptable, focusing strictly on the children's needs. This might include setting boundaries around the frequency of communication to prevent harassment.

- **Neutral Language**: Agree on a requirement for neutral language in all communications, potentially including examples of acceptable and unacceptable language to guide interactions.

Structured Decision-Making

Decisions regarding the children's welfare can become battlegrounds. To prevent this, the co-parenting plan should specify:

- **Areas of Sole and Joint Decision-Making**: Delineate which types of decisions each parent can make independently and which require consultation. This clarity can reduce instances of unilateral decision-making that may lead to conflict.

- **Decision-Making Process**: For decisions that require joint consultation, outline a step-by-step process, including how disagreements will be resolved, possibly incorporating a neutral mediator if consensus cannot be reached.

Anticipating and Managing Conflict

Given the potential for high conflict, the co-parenting plan should proactively address how disputes are managed:

- **Conflict Resolution Strategies**: Incorporate strategies such as a cooling-off period, during which decisions are postponed until both parties can approach the issue more calmly.

- **Use of Mediators**: Identify situations where a mediator, GAL, and/or lawyer involvement might be beneficial, specifying how and when to engage mediation services.

Financial Arrangements

Financial obligations often become a point of contention. To mitigate this, include:

- **Transparent Accounting**: Use of shared online tools for tracking child-related expenses can ensure both parents have access to up-to-date financial information.

- **Regular Reviews**: Schedule annual reviews of financial contributions and expenses related to the children, allowing for adjustments based on changes in financial circumstances or the children's needs.

Flexibility for the Children's Sake

Children's needs evolve, and the co-parenting plan must adapt accordingly. This flexibility is even more crucial when one parent exhibits narcissistic tendencies, as their cooperation may vary over time. Including provisions for regular review and adjustment of the co-parenting plan can ensure it remains relevant and effective. These reviews are opportunities to reassess the plan's current functionality and make necessary modifications to support the children's changing needs and interests.

Protective Measures for High-Conflict Situations

In high-conflict dynamics, protective measures within the co-parenting plan can offer a buffer for the children and the non-narcissistic parent:

- **Safety Protocols**: In extreme cases, establish safety protocols for the children and the non-narcissistic parent, including conditions under which supervised visitation might be necessary.

- **Emergency Response Plan**: Outline a clear emergency response plan detailing steps to be taken in crises to ensure the children's safety and well-being.

Supporting the Children's Relationship with Both Parents

Despite the challenges, it's vital to encourage a positive relationship between the children and both parents. The co-parenting plan should:

- **Encourage Positive Talk**: Commit to speaking positively—or at least neutrally—about the other parent in the children's presence.

- **Facilitate Quality Time**: Ensure the co-parenting schedule allows for meaningful engagement with both parents, respecting the children's desires and comfort levels.

Documentation and Legal Considerations

Given the potential for disagreements or disputes, documenting and incorporating the co-parenting plan into the legal custody agreement can provide security and enforceability. This documentation serves as a reference point for both parents, offering clarity and reducing the likelihood of misunderstandings.

In integrating these tailored strategies into your co-parenting plan, the goal is to create a framework that not only meets the logistical and emotional needs of co-parenting with a narcissistic ex but also prioritizes the well-being and stability of the children above all else. By anticipating potential challenges and incorporating mechanisms to manage them effectively, this customized co-parenting plan serves as a dynamic blueprint for navigating the complexities of raising children in a high-conflict co-parenting arrangement.

USING MEDIATION TO FACILITATE AGREEMENT

In the realm of co-parenting, especially when one parent exhibits narcissistic traits, achieving a mutually beneficial agreement can sometimes feel unobtainable. Here, mediation is a structured process aimed at bridging divides. This segment explores how mediation can be a critical instrument in formulating a co-parenting plan that respects both parent's perspectives while keeping the children's best interests at the forefront.

The Role of a Mediator

Mediation involves a neutral third party, the mediator, facilitating discussions between co-parents. Unlike a judge, a mediator doesn't make decisions but helps parents find common ground. They guide the conversation, ensuring that both voices are heard and valued. This approach is particularly effective when direct communication might lead to conflict or power imbalances that could hinder open dialogue.

- **Neutral Space**: The mediator creates a safe, neutral environment for discussions, away from the emotional charges of past shared spaces.

- **Structured Process**: They keep the conversation focused and on track, using structured techniques to explore options and test solutions.

- **Expertise and Experience**: With a background in conflict resolution, mediators bring a wealth of strategies designed to address the complexities of co-parenting dynamics.

Benefits of Mediation in Co-Parenting

When co-parenting with a narcissistic ex, the benefits of mediation extend beyond the immediate goal of reaching an agreement. This process can transform how parents interact, laying a foundation for more positive communication.

- **Reduced Conflict**: By focusing on problem-solving rather than blame, mediation can lower the temperature of interactions, reducing the potential for future conflicts.

- **Empowerment**: Parents often feel more invested in agreements they've had a hand in crafting. Mediation empowers both parties, giving them a sense of control over the outcome.

- **Flexibility**: Unlike court orders, mediation outcomes can be highly customized to fit the family's unique needs, offering practical and creative solutions.

- **Cost-Effectiveness**: Mediation can be more cost-effective than litigation, saving parents both the financial and emotional expense of court proceedings.

- **Preservation of Relationships**: By promoting respectful communication and mutual understanding, mediation can help preserve the co-parenting relationship, benefiting the children in the long run.

Preparing for Mediation

Preparation is critical to maximizing the chances of a successful mediation. This involves reading oneself emotionally and gathering the necessary information and insights to contribute effectively to the discussion.

- **Set Clear Goals**: Understand what you hope to achieve through mediation. This clarity will help you stay focused during discussions.

- **Gather Documentation**: Bring all relevant documents to the mediation process, such as communication logs, children's schedules, or previous agreements.

- **Reflect on Flexibility Points**: Identify areas where you're willing to compromise and those where you need to stand firm, understanding that flexibility often leads to more favorable outcomes.

During Mediation

The mediation session is a structured opportunity to work toward a mutually acceptable co-parenting plan. Here are some strategies to ensure the process is as productive as possible.

- **Listen Actively**: Give your full attention when your ex-partner speaks. Understanding their perspective, even if you disagree, can provide valuable insights.

- **Use 'I' Statements**: Speak from your own experience to reduce defensiveness. For example, "I feel overwhelmed when..." instead of "You always..."

- **Stay Child-Focused**: Keep the conversation centered on the children's needs. This shared priority can often be a unifying factor.

- **Take Breaks if Needed**: Don't hesitate to request a short break to regroup and refocus if emotions run high.

After Mediation

Following a successful mediation, it's important to formalize the agreement to ensure that both parties are clear on their commitments.

- **Written Agreement**: Have the mediator draft a written version of the agreed-upon co-parenting plan during the session. This document should detail the responsibilities, schedules, and communication protocols decided upon.

- **Legal Review**: Consider having a lawyer review the agreement to ensure it's in line with legal standards and to explore if it should be submitted to the court for official approval.

- **Implementation Plan**: Develop a clear plan for putting the agreement into action. This might involve setting up shared calendars, downloading co-parenting apps, or scheduling follow-up meetings to review how the arrangement works.

Mediation can offer a path away from conflict and towards cooperation, emphasizing problem-solving, mutual respect, and, above all, the well-being of the children involved. Through this process, parents can move beyond their differences, crafting a co-parenting plan to serve as a solid foundation for their new family dynamics.

ADJUSTING THE CO-PARENTING PLAN AS CHILDREN GROW

As children evolve from one stage of development to the next, their needs, interests, and routines also change. This dynamic shift necessitates that the co-parenting plan devised with your ex-partner, who displays narcissistic behaviors, must not remain static. It should be a living document, flexible enough to adapt to the maturing needs of your children. This approach ensures that the parenting strategy continues to serve the best interests of your children, providing them with the stability and support they need at every age.

Recognizing Signs for Revision

Significant changes in the children's lives often prompt adjustments to the co-parenting plan. These can include transitioning to a new school level, developing new interests or health needs, or changes in the living situation of either parent. Both parents must remain attentive to these signs of change, understanding that the original co-parenting plan, while effective at one point, may no longer fully address the current needs of their children.

- **Academic Changes**: As children progress in school, their academic commitments and extracurricular activities become more demanding. This can necessitate adjustments in the co-parenting schedule to accommodate these new responsibilities.

- **Social Development**: Children's social circles expand with age, and they begin to value spending time with peers. The co-parenting plan may need flexibility for social activities, sleepovers, and birthday parties.

- **Health and Well-being**: Any changes in a child's health or emotional well-being should prompt a review of the co-parenting plan. This ensures that both parents are aligned in their approach to healthcare, mental health support, and any necessary accommodations.

Engaging in Productive Dialogue

When it becomes apparent that the co-parenting plan requires revision, initiating a productive dialogue with your ex-partner is the next step. This conversation should focus on the children's evolving needs, aiming to keep personal differences aside for their benefit.

- **Prepare Your Points**: Before the discussion, list the specific reasons why you believe adjustments are needed, focusing on concrete examples that illustrate how your children's needs have changed.

- **Seek Common Ground**: Approach the conversation to find solutions that benefit the children, aiming to find common ground with your ex-partner despite past conflicts.

Incorporating Children's Voices

As children grow, they develop their own opinions and preferences about their living arrangements and schedules. Their voices need to be heard and considered in revising the co-parenting plan. This respects their growing autonomy and ensures the plan aligns with their needs and desires.

- **Age-Appropriate Discussions**: Have open conversations with your children about their wishes, ensuring that these discussions are age-appropriate and that children understand the goal is to support their best interests.

- **Balancing Preferences with Needs**: While children's preferences should be considered, it's also crucial to balance these with their overall needs for stability, education, and well-being.

Utilizing Professional Assistance

Adjusting a co-parenting plan, especially in situations involving a narcissistic ex-partner, can be complex. Seeking professional assistance from mediators, child psychologists, A GAL, or lawyers can provide the support needed to navigate these adjustments successfully.

- **Mediation Services**: A mediator can facilitate discussions between co-parents, helping to reach an agreement that reflects the children's evolving needs.

- **Child Development Experts**: Consulting with child psychologists or development experts can offer insights into what adjustments may benefit the children at different stages of their growth.

Implementing and Reviewing Adjustments

Once an agreement is reached on the necessary adjustments, the revised co-parenting plan should be implemented with clear communication and consistency. It's also vital to establish a process for regularly reviewing the plan, ensuring it continues to meet the children's needs over time.

- **Document Changes**: Any adjustments to the co-parenting plan should be documented in writing, with both parents signing and retaining a copy. This ensures clarity and accountability.

- **Scheduled Reviews**: Set regular intervals for reviewing the co-parenting plan, such as annually or during significant life transitions, to assess its effectiveness and make further adjustments.

The essence of a successful co-parenting plan lies in its ability to adapt to the changing landscape of your children's lives. By staying attuned to their needs, engaging in open dialogue with your ex-partner, and seeking professional guidance, you can ensure that the co-parenting plan remains a solid foundation for your children's growth and well-being. This flexible approach not only supports the diverse needs of your children through different stages of their development but also fosters a co-parenting relationship that prioritizes their best interests above all.

Chapter 8

Rebuilding and Finding Happiness Post-Divorce

T he ink dries on the divorce papers, and suddenly, the world seems vast and intimidating. You stand at a crossroads, with the path behind you a narrative of what was and the roads ahead brimming with possibilities of what could be. While daunting, this moment also promises growth, renewal, and happiness. The end of a marriage or relationship, particularly one entangled with narcissism, can feel like an unraveling. Yet, personal growth occurs within this space, and you can create a positive future for yourself.

STRATEGIES FOR MAKING A POSITIVE HOME AFTER DIVORCE

Embrace the Power of Reflection

You have ended your marriage/relationship with the narcissist, the parent of your children. Whether you have decided to co-parent or parallel parent to raise your children, you can now move forward and devote some time to creating your new family home environment. This effort goes beyond simply maintaining routines; it's about actively creating an environment where joy, love, and security flourish, allowing your children to adjust and find happiness amidst change. You need to rebuild yourself and your environment not only for your children but also for yourself. A strong, dynamic, vibrant, and happy you will benefit all of you.

Prioritizing Emotional Safety

First and foremost, emotional safety is the foundation upon which a positive home environment is built. Children need to feel heard, seen, and valued, free to express their thoughts and emotions without fear of judgment or dismissal. This begins with regular, open conversations where they can share their feelings about the divorce and any changes to their family dynamics.

- Encourage daily check-ins, using mealtimes or bedtimes as opportunities for discussion.

- Introduce emotion charts or journals for younger children to help them articulate their feelings.

Maintaining Consistency

The whirlwind of divorce disrupts the familiar, making consistency in the home more crucial than ever. Strive to keep daily routines intact, from mealtimes and bedtimes to after-school activities. This consistency provides a sense of normalcy and security, serving as a reminder that some things remain unchanged despite the upheaval.

- Create visual schedules for younger children to help them understand and anticipate daily and weekly routines.

- Involve older children in planning their schedules, empowering them with control.

Creating a Space of Belonging

Every child needs a sanctuary, a space to feel utterly at ease. In a post-divorce home, ensuring each child has a space that reflects their personality and interests is key. This might mean redecorating their room to match their current passions or setting aside a corner of the living room for their crafts or books.

- Involve children in personalizing their spaces, from paint colors to decorations.

- Establish family spaces with photos and memorabilia that celebrate happy memories and milestones.

Fostering Open Communication

Divorce can lead to questions, many of which children might hesitate to ask. Fostering an environment where open communication is encouraged and celebrated ensures they never feel alone with their thoughts. This involves being available, attentive, and ready to listen and respond honestly and empathetically.

- Set aside regular family meetings where everyone can voice their thoughts, concerns, and suggestions.

- Use storybooks or movies dealing with themes of change and resilience as conversation starters.

Encouraging Positive Experiences

Building positive experiences helps counterbalance the stress and sadness divorce can bring. This doesn't necessitate grand gestures; instead, it's about seizing the joy in the everyday. Ordinary things like cooking together, watching a movie together, weekend nature walks, or evening board games can all serve as reminders of the love and happiness that bind the family together.

- Plan regular "adventure days" where each child gets to choose an activity for the family to enjoy together.

- Start new traditions that celebrate your family's resilience and unity, such as a monthly gratitude jar.

Supporting Social Connections

A strong support network of friends and extended family members is pivotal in a child's adjustment post-divorce/separation. Encourage children to maintain and cultivate these relationships, providing opportunities for social interaction outside the immediate family.

- Coordinate playdates or sleepovers with friends, offering a sense of continuity in their social lives.

- Facilitate regular visits, or Facetime calls with extended family members, reinforcing the network of love and support surrounding them.

Promoting Resilience Through Role Modeling

Children learn resilience not just through words but through witnessing it in action. By navigating the post-divorce landscape with strength, optimism, and a willingness to seek joy and growth, you will model resilience, and your children will pick up on this. This means embracing change, celebrating progress, and showing kindness and forgiveness to oneself and others.

- Share stories of personal challenges and how you overcame them, highlighting the lessons learned.

- Demonstrate self-care practices, teaching children the importance of looking after their mental and physical well-being.

Navigating Challenges with Empathy and Respect

Despite the best intentions, challenges are inevitable as the family home changes and loyalties are tested. It's essential to handle these moments with empathy and respect, always prioritizing the emotional well-being of the children.

- When conflicts arise, address them directly but gently, striving for solutions that respect everyone's feelings and needs.

- Be mindful of the children's loyalty bonds. They may feel torn between their affection for their biological parent and their growing attachment to their "new life" without that parent living in the same house. Reassure them that it's okay to be happy in their "new home" without the other parent living with them.

- Continue to use your co-parenting or parallel parenting plan for all parental decisions and household rules. Consistency in these areas provides stability and clarity for the children.

CELEBRATING SMALL VICTORIES: A PATH TO RENEWAL

In the aftermath of divorce, especially from a partnership marked by narcissism, the landscape of life can seem daunting, filled with challenges both big and small. However, amidst this, there lies an opportunity for growth and healing, often found in recognizing and celebrating the small victories that occur along the way. These moments, seemingly inconsequential on the surface, are the basis of a newfound sense of self and a life reclaimed from the shadows of a traumatic past.

Embracing Self-Compassion

Self-compassion is a crucial element in celebrating small victories. Post-divorce can be fraught with self-doubt and criticism, particularly in situations where you're rebuilding from a narcissistic relationship. Treating yourself and your children with kindness and understanding fosters a supportive internal environment where victories, no matter how small, can be fully appreciated. Your children are always watching you and will model your behavior; teach them the importance of good self-care.

- Practice mindfulness and positive self-talk. Counter negative thoughts with reminders of your strengths and the progress you've made.

- Allow yourself to feel pride in your accomplishments without minimizing them. Remember, every step forward is a victory in its own right.

Finding Joy in the Everyday

This means shifting focus from what's been lost to the opportunities and pleasures that now lie before you. Help your kids to make this shift and focus on the new opportunities ahead for the family. It could be the simple joy of a quiet morning; the laughter shared with a friend or the satisfaction of completing a task. These moments contribute to a growing sense of happiness and fulfillment when acknowledged and celebrated.

- Make it a habit to identify at least one thing that brought you joy or satisfaction each day. Reflect on why it was meaningful and how it contributed to your day. Try to get your kids to do this as well.

- Engage in and encourage your kids to engage in activities that bring you happiness, whether a creative hobby, exercise, or time in nature. Celebrate the freedom to pursue these interests on your terms.

Cultivating Gratitude

Cultivating a mindset of gratitude goes hand in hand with celebrating small victories. By focusing on the positives in your life, including your progress and personal growth, you reinforce a positive outlook that supports continued healing and development. This is so important for your family.

- Keep a gratitude journal where you and the kids list daily things you're thankful for. Keep it someplace central where the kids will be sure to see it, like in the kitchen. If your kids are young, make a rainbow of gratitude. Go to the store and buy a few sheets of colored construction paper (red, orange, yellow, green, blue, purple). Cut them into long, thin strips, ask your kids for something they are grateful for, and write them down on different strips. Then, together, you can build a rainbow and hang it on the fridge; it will be a nice visual reminder for them.

- Express gratitude to those who support you, whether through a simple thank you, a note, or a gesture of appreciation. Let your kids see you doing this, and explain what you are doing. Recognizing the role of others in your journey highlights the interconnected web of support that surrounds you. and the kids. This will make the kids feel very grounded, secure, and supported.

Celebrating small victories on the path to post-divorce renewal is not just about marking milestones; it's about redefining your journey regarding growth, resilience, and the capacity to find joy and meaning in the tapestry of everyday life. It's a practice that boosts morale and encourages optimism and gratitude, laying the foundation for a future filled with potential and happiness.

FUTURE PROOFING YOUR FAMILY AGAINST NARCISSISTIC INFLUENCE

In the aftermath of a divorce, particularly one involving a partner with narcissistic traits, the echoes of influence can linger, subtly shaping the dynamics of your family. It becomes paramount, then, to put measures in place that not only shield your family from these remnants of influence but also fortify the emotional and psychological resilience of your loved ones. This proactive stance is not about building walls but rather about nurturing an environment where the well-being and stability of your family are safeguarded.

Building Emotional Resilience in Your Children

Children, with their remarkable adaptability, also possess a vulnerability to the undercurrents of emotional manipulation. Future-proofing them against such influence involves teaching them to recognize and articulate their emotions, understand boundaries, and critically assess interactions and relationships.

- **Critical Thinking Skills**: Engage your children in discussions, encouraging them to think critically about interactions and relationships. Use age-appropriate examples from books or movies to illustrate healthy versus unhealthy dynamics.

- **Emotionally Expressive**: Create a home environment where emotions can be freely expressed and discussed. Utilize activities like art or storytelling to help younger children express complex feelings.

Strengthening Your Support Network

A robust support network acts as a buffer, absorbing shocks and stresses that might otherwise impact your family. It's about surrounding yourself and your children with individuals who bring positivity, offer support, and understand the nuances of your situation. This network can include close friends, family members, and professionals like therapists or counselors.

- **Community Involvement**: Encourage involvement in community activities or groups that align with your family's interests. This can broaden your support network and introduce you to others with similar experiences.

- **Professional Guidance**: Regular sessions with a therapist familiar with narcissistic behaviors can provide your family with strategies to deal with lingering influences and foster healthy emotional development.

Educating Yourself and Your Family

Knowledge is a powerful tool in recognizing and counteracting narcissistic influence. Educating yourself and your family about narcissism, including its manifestations and the ways it can impact individuals and relationships, is critical.

- **Family Discussions**: Hold open discussions about the importance of respect, empathy, and boundaries in relationships. Tailor the conversation to be age-appropriate, ensuring it's constructive and not fear-inducing.

- **Resources and Reading**: Compile a list of resources, books, and articles that offer insights into narcissism and emotional resilience. Consider reading a book together as a family and discussing its themes.

Promoting Independence and Self-Efficacy

Encouraging independence and a sense of self-efficacy in your children helps them build confidence in their abilities and decisions. This empowerment is a crucial defense against external influences that seek to undermine their autonomy.

- **Decision-Making Opportunities**: Give your children age-appropriate opportunities to decide about weekend activities or more significant choices like extracurricular interests.

- **Problem-Solving Skills**: Work through everyday challenges together, guiding your children in brainstorming solutions and evaluating outcomes. This process helps them develop critical problem-solving skills and reliance on their judgment.

Maintaining Open Lines of Communication

Ensuring that lines of communication remain open and honest within your family is essential. This openness fosters an environment where concerns can be raised and issues addressed without fear of judgment or reprisal.

- **Regular Family Meetings**: Establish a routine of holding family meetings where everyone can share their thoughts, feelings, and concerns.

- **Active Listening**: Practice active listening, showing genuine interest and empathy in what your children and family members express. This validates their feelings and encourages them to share.

In implementing these strategies, the aim is not only to shield your family from the influence of a narcissistic ex-partner but also to cultivate an environment where growth, resilience, and emotional well-being are at the forefront. By building emotional resilience, strengthening your support network, educating your family, promoting independence, and maintaining open communication, you lay the groundwork for a future where your family can thrive despite past challenges.

As we move forward, it's crucial to remember that the scars left by narcissistic influence do not define your family's future. Instead, through proactive measures and a commitment to healing and growth, a new chapter awaits—one where stability, happiness, and resilience are not just aspirations but realities.

Chapter 9

Co-Parenting Across Cultures: Embracing Diversity

F amilies often find themselves at the crossroads of diverse cultural backgrounds in a smaller and more connected world than ever. This richness can add layers of complexity to co-parenting, especially when navigating the aftermath of a relationship with a narcissist. Here, the challenge isn't just about managing communication and logistics; it's about ensuring that the cultural heritage of both parents is respected and celebrated, providing a solid foundation for children's identities.

When cultures blend, so do parenting styles, traditions, and expectations. This amalgamation, while beautiful, requires careful navigation to foster an environment where children feel connected to their roots and where parents feel respected and heard. Unfortunately, often, the narcissistic ex will not cooperate in honoring culturing traditions that are not their own.

CULTURAL CONSIDERATIONS IN CO-PARENTING AND PARALLEL PARENTING

Families can be made up of traditions, beliefs, and practices that define their unique cultural identity. Recognizing and valuing these differences is not just a courtesy; it's necessary in crafting a co-parenting or parallel parenting plan that honors the backgrounds of both parents. This acknowledgment ensures that children grow up with a sense of belonging and an understanding of their heritage.

Understanding Cultural Norms and Their Impact on Parenting

Cultures have distinct views on parenting roles, discipline, education, and day-to-day activities. For instance, while one parent may prioritize academic excellence based on their cultural background, another might emphasize social development and community involvement. Understanding these differences is the first step toward finding common ground.

- **Open Dialogue**: Start with honest conversations about your cultural values and how they influence your parenting. This should include discussions on holidays, language, religious practices, and expectations around family roles.

- **Education and Exposure**: Take the time to learn about the different cultures contributing to your family. This can involve reading books, attending cultural events, or preparing traditional meals together. The goal is not just tolerance but appreciation and understanding.

- **Flexible Traditions**: Be willing to adapt and blend traditions. This might mean creating new holiday celebrations incorporating elements from both cultures or alternating between cultural traditions for significant events like birthdays.

Developing a Culturally Inclusive Parenting Plan

A parenting plan that respects both parents' cultural backgrounds provides children with a rich, diverse heritage. Here are some practical steps to ensure your plan is culturally inclusive:

- **Language**: If both parents speak different languages, include provisions for the child to learn and use both languages. This might involve attending language classes or spending time with family members who can speak the respective language.

- **Holidays and Traditions**: Decide how to celebrate cultural and religious holidays, ensuring children can experience both parents' traditions.

- **Dietary Considerations**: Include any cultural dietary restrictions or preferences in your parenting plan, ensuring that children are exposed to the cuisines of both cultures.

- **Educational Choices**: Make decisions about your child's education that reflect respect for both cultures. This could involve enrolling children in schools offering a diverse cultural curriculum or supporting learning both parents' languages.

- **Cultural Festivals and Events**: Make it a point to attend cultural festivals and events as a family. These outings are educational and fun, offering a firsthand experience of cultural traditions, foods, and arts.

NAVIGATING CULTURAL NORMS AND EXPECTATIONS WITH A NARCISSISTIC EX

Engaging with a narcissistic ex-partner over matters of cultural norms and expectations can be a challenging endeavor, especially when children's well-being and cultural identity are at stake. Ensuring that children benefit from their rich cultural heritage while safeguarding them from potential conflict requires a strategic and thoughtful approach.

Understanding the Dynamics

Before any meaningful dialogue can happen, it's vital to comprehend the dynamics at play when dealing with a narcissistic ex-partner. Their need for control and tendency to use emotional manipulation can significantly impact discussions about cultural upbringing. Recognizing these patterns is the first step in preparing to navigate these conversations effectively.

- Be aware of manipulation tactics that may be used to undermine cultural importance or to assert dominance in decision-making.

- Prepare for resistance to compromises that involve cultural practices different from their own or that they perceive as less valuable.

Strategic Communication

Effective communication becomes your most potent tool in these situations. The goal is not to change the narcissistic ex-partner's perspective but to establish clear and respectful boundaries around cultural norms and expectations for your children's upbringing.

- Opt for written communication for clarity and to maintain a record of agreements or discussions. Again, one of the co-parenting apps works best for this.

- Use neutral language focusing on the children's needs and well-being rather than personal differences.

Legal and Professional Resources

Sometimes, direct communication may not yield the desired outcomes, or it may not be safe to engage directly with the narcissistic ex-partner. In such cases, turning to legal and professional resources can provide the necessary framework to ensure children's cultural rights are respected.

- Consult with a family law attorney familiar with multicultural issues to understand your legal options and rights regarding cultural upbringing.

Empowering Children with Knowledge

An essential aspect of navigating cultural norms with a narcissistic ex involves empowering your children with knowledge about their cultural heritage. This not only strengthens their identity but also equips them with the understanding to appreciate the diversity in their family background.

- Introduce children to books, music, and art from both cultural backgrounds to foster an appreciation for their heritage.

- Encourage open discussions about culture and identity, allowing children to express their feelings and questions about their multicultural heritage.

Building a Supportive Community

Creating a supportive environment that celebrates cultural diversity can help mitigate the impact of a narcissistic ex's attempts to undermine cultural norms and expectations. Surrounding yourself and your children with a community that values multiculturalism ensures children grow up with a strong sense of identity and belonging. Navigating the cultural landscape with a narcissistic ex requires a delicate balance of assertiveness, diplomacy, and a steadfast commitment to the children's best interests. Through strategic communication, legal safeguards, and cultivating a supportive and inclusive environment, you can honor your children's heritage and ensure they grow up with a rich, multifaceted cultural identity.

Chapter 10

Navigating the Shadows: Understanding Covert Narcissism

I magine walking into a room blindfolded, with only your sense of hearing to guide you. You're trying to locate someone you've been told is right there with you, but their footsteps are silent, their breaths barely audible. This is akin to identifying and dealing with covert narcissism, especially in the context of co-parenting. Unlike its more overt counterpart, which announces itself with unmistakable arrogance and entitlement, covert narcissism lurks in the shadows; its presence is felt more in what isn't said than what is. It's the silence between words, the absence rather than the action, that often speaks volumes.

RECOGNIZING AND RESPONDING TO COVERT NARCISSISM

Identifying the Signs

Covert narcissism manifests in a lack of empathy disguised as sensitivity, in a need for admiration that masquerades as humility. Here are some signs:

- They tend to play the victim in various situations, especially when at fault.

- An understated sense of superiority, believing they are better than others but not necessarily showing it outright.

- Envying others' successes or possessions, often couched in passive-aggressive comments.

- A need for recognition and admiration that might not be overt but is persistent and pervasive.

Strategies for Co-Parenting with a Covert Narcissist

Dealing with a covert narcissist requires a blend of firmness and flexibility. You're aiming not to confront them but to work around their behaviors, keeping the well-being of your children at the forefront. Consider these approaches:

- **Setting Clear Boundaries**: This isn't about confrontation but clarity. Clearly outline what is acceptable and what isn't in your co-parenting arrangement. This might involve written communication for major decisions or using a third-party mediator for discussions.

- **Maintaining Emotional Distance**: Engage with them, focusing on facts rather than emotions. This might feel like you're always treading on eggshells, but it's about protecting your emotional health and ensuring your interactions are productive rather than destructive.

- **Documenting Interactions**: Keep a record of conversations and decisions. This isn't about "catching them out" but ensuring clarity on agreements made and providing a basis for resolving disputes.

- **Seeking Support**: Whether it's from friends, family, or professionals, having a support network is crucial. They can offer perspectives and advice, helping you to remain grounded.

LEGAL PROTECTIONS AGAINST HARASSMENT AND ABUSE

When the dynamics of co-parenting with a narcissist veer into the realms of harassment or abuse, safeguarding your peace and ensuring the safety of your children becomes paramount. It's not merely about navigating tricky waters anymore; it's about securing a lifeline in the storm. Here, we show you the path to obtaining legal protection, a process that, while daunting, stands as a bulwark against the storm of narcissistic abuse.

Understanding Your Rights and Legal Options

The first step in this crucial process involves a thorough understanding of what constitutes harassment and abuse in the eyes of the law. It's important to recognize that emotional and psychological abuse, often wielded by narcissists, is taken seriously by legal systems today. Familiarizing yourself with the specific statutes in your jurisdiction can empower you to take decisive action.

- **Consultation with a Family Law Attorney**: An experienced attorney can clarify the legal definitions of harassment and abuse and advise on the most appropriate course of action based on your situation.

- **Legal Orders of Protection**: Often referred to as restraining orders, these legal documents can limit a narcissist's behavior and interactions with you and your children, offering a layer of safety and peace.

Gathering and Presenting Evidence

In legal proceedings, evidence is king. It substantiates your claims and paints a vivid picture of the covert narcissist's behavior for the court. Collecting this evidence requires diligence and attention to detail.

- **Documenting Instances of Harassment or Abuse**: Keep a detailed record of interactions, including dates, times, and descriptions of incidents. Text messages, emails, and voicemails can serve as evidence of harassment or psychological abuse. Again, using a co-parenting app to document and keep track of all of this is very helpful. Remember to find out which parenting apps are accepted by your local courts.

- **Witness Statements**: If others have witnessed abusive or harassing behavior, their written statements can support your case. This might include friends, family members, or even professionals like therapists or teachers who have observed the effects of the narcissist's behavior on you or your children.

- **Police Reports:** If your ex's behavior is egregious enough, call the police and file a report. Get the interaction documented and ensure the police can access any witness to the episode. Even if there is not enough information to bring charges against your ex, documenting abusive behavior by the police is a strong paper trail your narcissistic ex will not be able to manipulate.

Navigating the Legal Process

Armed with knowledge and evidence, the next step involves utilizing the legal process to secure protection. This, unfortunately, is not simple, but it can be done. It will require diligence, determination, and patience and be a testament to your resilience and commitment to safeguarding your family.

- **Filing for an Order of Protection**: This generally involves completing detailed forms and submitting them to a court. While the process can vary from jurisdiction to jurisdiction, family law attorneys can guide you through it, ensuring all necessary documentation is correctly filed.

- **The Court Hearing**: Should your case go to a hearing, being prepared is vital. This includes organizing evidence, understanding what to expect during the hearing, and presenting your case effectively. Again, legal representation can be invaluable in this setting, providing you with the advocacy needed to navigate court proceedings confidently.

Support Systems and Self-Care

Remembering to care for yourself and leaning on your support system is vital amid legal battles. The emotional toll of confronting a narcissist in court, coupled with the stress of the legal process, can be overwhelming.

- **Therapeutic Support**: Engaging with a therapist experienced in dealing with narcissistic abuse can provide you with coping strategies and emotional support during this challenging time.

- **Community Support**: Whether it's through support groups for survivors of narcissistic abuse or communities of individuals who have gone through similar legal struggles, finding solidarity with others who understand can be incredibly comforting.

Protecting Your Children

Throughout this process, the well-being of your children remains the highest priority. Ensuring they are shielded from the trauma of legal conflicts and safeguarded against the destabilizing effects of harassment and abuse is paramount.

- **Legal Advocacy for Children**: In some cases, the court may appoint a special advocate or GAL for your children, ensuring their best interests are represented throughout legal proceedings.

- **Open, Age-Appropriate Communication**: Keeping the lines of communication open with your children is crucial. Explaining the situation in terms they can understand, reassuring them of their safety, and reinforcing your love for them are key components of helping them navigate this period.

In seeking legal protections against harassment and abuse, you're not just pursuing a remedy for the present; you're laying the groundwork for a safer, more stable future for you and your children.

ADVANCED DOCUMENTATION TECHNIQUES FOR EXTREME CASES

In the realm of co-parenting with a narcissistic ex-partner, certain situations demand an even greater level of vigilance and preparedness. When the usual advice on keeping track of interactions feels insufficient due to the complexity or severity of the case, turning to advanced documentation techniques can provide the robust evidence needed for legal protection and custody negotiations. This approach is about creating a comprehensive and detailed record that can stand up to scrutiny in any legal setting, ensuring that the welfare of your children remains the top priority.

Emails and Texts: Beyond the Basics

While most are familiar with saving emails and texts, take this to the next level and delve into the nuances that can make these communications more effective as documentation. Consider these strategies:

- **Subject Lines as Summaries**: Use the subject line of emails to summarize the content. For example, "Request for Change in Weekend Visitation - June 5th."

This makes it easier to find specific communications later.

- **BCC Your Attorney**: When sending important emails, use the BCC function to include your attorney. This keeps them in the loop and ensures there's a secondary record of the communication.

- **Print and Store**: Regularly print out important texts and emails. Digital data can be lost or corrupted, so having a physical copy provides an additional layer of security.

Using Technology to Your Advantage

Several apps and software are designed specifically for co-parenting, offering features that can enhance your documentation efforts. These tools often include:

- **Integrated Messaging**: All communication can be conducted within the app, automatically saving and organizing messages for easy access.

- **Expense Tracking**: Provides a platform for logging and sharing expenses related to your children, complete with the ability to attach receipts and invoices.

- **Visit Logs**: Some apps offer features to log visitation, including dates, times, and notes about each visit, which can be invaluable in custody negotiations.

Voice Memos as a Tool

When it's important to remember specific conversations or incidents, voice memos can be an invaluable tool. After an interaction, take a moment to record a memo summarizing what was said or what occurred. These memos can serve as contemporaneous notes, providing a fresh and detailed account that can be transcribed and added to your digital logbook.

- **Always Date and Time**: Begin each voice memo with the date and time of the recording.

- **Be Specific**: Include specific details such as locations, what both parties said, and any actions taken. The more detail, the better.

Maintaining a Physical Evidence File

A digital copy may not suffice for certain types of evidence, or you may have physical items pertinent to your case. Maintaining a physical evidence file in a safe and organized manner is crucial. This could include:

- **Legal Documents**: Copies of your case's legal filings, court orders, or official correspondence.

- **Physical Correspondence**: Letters, cards, or notes that may be relevant to your situation.

- **Educational Records**: Report cards, letters from teachers, or records of parent-teacher conferences that highlight the involvement (or lack thereof) of the narcissistic co-parent in your child's education.

Engaging with Professionals

Sometimes, the situation's complexity may warrant professional assistance in gathering and organizing documentation. Private investigators or legal professionals can offer services that ensure your documentation is thorough, relevant, and legally admissible. They can also guide you on the ethical and legal considerations of collecting certain types of evidence.

- **Consult Before Acting**: Always consult with your attorney before engaging a professional investigator, especially if you're considering surveillance or other sensitive methods of evidence collection.

- **Professional Organization**: For complex cases, legal professionals can assist in organizing your evidence, ensuring that it's presented in the most effective manner possible.

In extreme situations where the usual documentation methods may not be sufficient, these advanced techniques offer a way to build a comprehensive and compelling case. Whether leveraging technology, engaging with professionals, or meticulously organizing physical and digital records, the goal remains to protect your children and safeguard their well-being in legal proceedings.

CRISIS MANAGEMENT: IMMEDIATE STEPS WHEN CHILDREN ARE AT RISK

In moments when the safety and emotional well-being of children become compromised due to the actions of a narcissistic ex-partner, acting swiftly and decisively is paramount. The unpredictability of a narcissist's behavior necessitates a deliberate plan of action, ensuring that parents are equipped to respond effectively to protect their children. This section outlines practical steps and considerations for managing crises, highlighting the importance of preparedness in safeguarding the most vulnerable victims of narcissistic behavior.

Preparation: The Keystone of Crisis Management

The foundation of effective crisis management lies in preparation. Anticipating potential scenarios that might arise allows parents to respond with confidence and precision. This preparation involves:

- **Emergency Contacts**: Compile a list of essential contacts, including law enforcement, child protective services, trusted legal counsel, and supportive family members or friends. Having these contacts readily available can save precious time in an emergency.

- **Safety Plan**: Develop a safety plan with your children tailored to their age and comprehension level. This should include safe places they can go, trusted adults they can turn to, and rehearsed responses to various scenarios.

- **Legal Documentation**: Keep copies of any relevant legal documents, such as restraining orders, custody agreements, or documented evidence of the narcissistic ex-partner's behavior, in a secure, quickly accessible location. Digital copies stored in a secure cloud service can provide an additional layer of preparedness.

Recognizing the Signs: When to Act

Understanding the signals of escalating behavior in a narcissistic ex-partner is critical in preempting potential crises. These signs might include:

- **Increased Aggression or Threats**: Take note of any uptick in aggressive communication or explicit threats. These can be harbingers of more severe actions to come.

- **Unpredictable Behavior**: Sudden, inexplicable changes in behavior or patterns of interaction can indicate a shift towards a more volatile state.

- **Manipulation of Children**: Be vigilant for signs that the narcissistic ex-partner is attempting to manipulate or turn the children against you, as this can signify a move to undermine your authority or destabilize their emotional well-being.

Immediate Actions: Safeguarding Your Children

When a crisis emerges, the priority is your children's immediate safety and emotional security. This includes:

- **Remove the Child from Harm's Way**: If the situation allows, removing the child from the immediate vicinity or influence of the narcissistic ex-partner is the first step. This might mean going to a predetermined safe space or the home of a trusted family member or friend.

- **Contact Authorities**: If there is any threat to physical safety, contacting law enforcement or child protective services is essential. They are equipped to handle such situations and can provide the necessary protection and intervention.

- **Activate Your Support Network**: Reach out to your support network for help. This can include family, friends, or professionals who can offer assistance, whether providing a safe place to stay, accompanying you to legal appointments, or simply being there to provide emotional support.

- **Consult with Legal Counsel**: If the crisis has legal implications, such as violations of a custody agreement or restraining order, consulting with your attorney can guide your next steps. They can advise on immediate legal actions to protect your children and uphold your rights.

Emotional Support: Navigating the Aftermath

In the wake of a crisis, attending to the emotional needs of your children is as crucial as addressing their physical safety. Consider the following approaches:

- **Reassurance**: Reassure your children and affirm their safety. Let them know that the steps taken were in their best interest and that they are now in a secure environment.

- **Professional Support**: Engaging the services of a child psychologist or therapist who specializes in dealing with trauma can be invaluable. They can provide your children with coping strategies and help them process their experiences healthily.

- **Open Communication**: Encourage your children to express their feelings and concerns. Listen actively and validate their emotions, offering them a safe space to voice their fears and anxieties.

Review and Reflect

Review the events and your response after the immediate crisis has been managed. Reflecting on what occurred can provide insights into how to strengthen your crisis management plan, ensuring you are better prepared for any future incidents. This reflection should include:

- **Evaluating the Effectiveness of Your Response**: Consider what actions were effective and what could be improved. This might involve strengthening your safety plan, updating emergency contacts, or seeking additional legal protections.

- **Learning from the Experience**: Every crisis presents a learning opportunity. Reflect on the sequence of events and your response to identify any gaps in your preparedness or areas where additional resources or support might be needed.

- **Strengthening Your Support Network**: The aftermath of a crisis can underscore the importance of a robust support network. Look for ways to expand and strengthen your network by connecting with other parents in similar situations, engaging with community resources, or seeking professional support services.

Facing a crisis caused by a narcissistic ex-partner's behavior is undoubtedly one of the most challenging aspects of co-parenting. However, with a well-prepared crisis management plan, a clear understanding of when and how to act, and a focus on the emotional well-being of your children, you can manage. Remember, in moments of crisis, your strength, preparedness, and unwavering commitment to your children's safety and security are their greatest allies.

LONG-TERM STRATEGIES FOR PROTECTING YOUR FAMILY

When dealing with a narcissistic parent, be proactive in setting your family up for peace and security in the long term.

Building Emotional Resilience in Your Children

At the heart of long-term protection lies the emotional resilience of your children. It's about giving them the tools to weather the storm and emerge unscathed, secure, and happy. This involves:

- **Regular Conversations**: Engage in ongoing dialogues about feelings, teaching them it's okay to express joy and distress. It's these conversations that lay the foundation for emotional intelligence.

- **Problem-Solving Skills**: Encourage them to think through problems, big or small, and develop solutions. This doesn't mean they're on their own; instead, it's about empowering them with the confidence to face challenges head-on, knowing they have your support.

- **Positive Affirmations**: Introduce them to the power of positive affirmations. They can say simple statements to themselves to boost their self-esteem and remind them of their inner strength and worth.

Educational Continuity and Support

The upheaval often associated with narcissistic co-parenting can disrupt a child's education. Ensuring continuity and support in their educational journey is a key long-term strategy. This can be achieved by:

- **Open Communication with Schools**: Keep an open line of communication with your children's teachers and school counselors. Inform them of any home situations that may affect your child's performance or behavior at school.

Extracurricular Activities: Encourage children to participate in

extracurricular activities that interest them, providing a constructive outlet for their energies and emotions.

Raising children with a narcissist is very difficult and demands vigilance on your part. Remember, do not react, do not engage in the drama, hold steady and stay calm. Be the constant in your children's lives, the one they can always count on, and they will thrive.

In moving forward, we carry with us the tools and knowledge we've gathered, ready to apply them not just in the context of co-parenting with a narcissistic ex but in all areas of our lives. The strategies outlined here are not just about survival; they're about thriving, turning adversity into strength, and building a family legacy of resilience and love

Chapter 11

Leveraging Technology for Smoother Co-Parenting

T he main argument here is straightforward: technology provides powerful tools that can significantly ease the challenges of co-parenting. This is especially true in cases where one parent is a narcissist. The boundaries, safeguards, and documentation technology provides are sheer gold. From apps that consolidate communication and scheduling to platforms that facilitate dispute resolution, the digital age presents solutions that past generations could only dream of.

COMMUNICATION MADE EASY

Remember when passing messages through children or waiting days for a response was the norm? Today, numerous apps offer secure, instant communication tailored for co-parenting. Features, like read receipts, eliminate the guesswork of whether a message has been seen, while built-in calendars allow for real-time updates to shared parenting schedules. This immediacy and transparency can drastically reduce misunderstandings and the stress that comes with them.

- Example: Consider an app like TalkingParents or CoParenter, which keeps communication records and provides mediation and dispute resolution tools, all within the same platform.

Scheduling Without the Hassle

Synchronizing schedules can be a logistical nightmare, especially with school events, medical appointments, and extracurricular activities. Co-parenting apps with shared calendars allow both parents to add, view, and manage appointments and events in real time. This ensures that both parents are informed, making negotiating changes or swaps in visitation times more straightforward.

Dispute Resolution at Your Fingertips

It's an uncomfortable truth that disputes are part of the co-parenting landscape, especially when dealing with a narcissistic co-parent. However, technology offers innovative solutions here, too. Online mediation services provide a platform for resolving conflicts without needing face-to-face confrontation. These platforms often employ certified mediators who guide the discussion, ensuring both parties are heard and working towards a mutually agreeable solution.

Safety and Privacy Concerns

While the benefits are numerous, it's essential to approach these digital tools with an awareness of privacy and security. Not all apps are created equal, and choosing platforms with robust security measures is crucial to protect sensitive information. Additionally, respecting the privacy of the co-parenting relationship and avoiding oversharing on social media platforms is key to maintaining a healthy digital co-parenting environment.

In conclusion, today's technology offers tools to make co-parenting more manageable, transparent, and conflict-free; this can often be the solution high-conflict co-patents desperately need. By carefully selecting and utilizing these technological solutions, parents can eliminate or reduce the amount of time spent with their ex, drastically reduce conflicts and hostile interactions, and focus less on the logistics of co-parenting and more on what matters most: raising happy, healthy children in a cooperative and respectful environment.

INNOVATIVE LEGAL SOLUTIONS FOR CO-PARENTING DISPUTES

In family law, strategies are evolving, adapting to the needs of modern families and the complexities of co-parenting arrangements. This evolution has led to innovative legal solutions designed to resolve co-parenting disputes, focusing on cases where parallel parenting and contentious relationships exist, all while prioritizing the well-being of the children involved. These solutions offer a fresh perspective on dispute resolution, moving away from the adversarial approach traditionally associated with family law and towards a more workable and constructive methodology.

Parenting Coordination

Another innovative solution is parenting coordination, a child-focused alternative dispute resolution process. Parenting coordinators are trained professionals, often with backgrounds in law, psychology, or social work, who assist high-conflict co-parents in implementing their parenting plan. The role of the parenting coordinator includes:

- Mediating Disputes: They mediate disagreements regarding the parenting plan, from minor scheduling conflicts to more significant disputes about education or healthcare decisions.

- Educating Parents: Coordinators also educate parents on how to communicate more effectively and make decisions that are in the best interest of their children.

- Making Recommendations: In some cases, with the parents' consent, coordinators can make binding decisions to resolve disputes quickly.

Online Dispute Resolution Platforms

Online dispute resolution (ODR) platforms have emerged as a convenient and efficient tool for resolving co-parenting disputes. The most widely used online dispute resolution platforms are:

Immediation, ADR Notable, Custody X Change, and Online Dispute Resolution by Modria

Not all of these platforms are used exclusively for co-parenting and child custody issues, but presently, these are the ones most widely used by lawyers practicing family law.

These platforms offer a variety of services, including:

- Virtual Mediation: Facilitated by experienced mediators, virtual mediation sessions allow co-parents to negotiate settlements from their homes.

- Document Preparation: Some platforms offer services to help parents prepare legal documents based on their mediated agreements, streamlining the process of formalizing their settlement.

Legal Apps and Tools

Various apps and digital tools have been developed to assist co-parents in managing their legal obligations and disputes. These tools offer various functionalities:

- Legal Document Generation: Parents can generate legally binding agreements related to their co-parenting arrangement, including custody schedules and financial support agreements.

- Record Keeping: Digital tools allow parents to keep detailed records of communication, expenses, and compliance with the parenting plan, which can be invaluable in a dispute.

- Dispute Logging: Some apps provide a feature for logging disputes, including attempts at resolution, which can be helpful if legal intervention becomes necessary.

The legal field's embrace of these innovative solutions reflects a growing recognition of the importance of resolving co-parenting disputes in a safe and structured manner that preserves family relationships and supports the best interests of the children involved.

NEW THERAPEUTIC APPROACHES FOR FAMILIES AFFECTED BY NARCISSISM

The landscape of therapy is ever-evolving, especially in its approach to aiding families entangled in the web of narcissistic dynamics. Traditional therapy has offered a foundational understanding and coping mechanisms for those dealing with narcissists. However, the nuanced challenges of co-parenting with a narcissist require innovative therapeutic strategies. These new approaches not only aim to heal but also empower families, providing them with the tools to navigate the intricate dance of relationships marked by narcissism.

Dynamic Family Therapy

Dynamic family therapy emerges as a modality for families caught in narcissistic abuse while attempting to co-parent with a narcissist. This approach shifts focus from individual therapy sessions to engaging the family as a whole. The aim is to foster healthier, safer communication, move forward, and repair the emotional damage inflicted by narcissistic behaviors. Here's how it unfolds:

- Interactive Sessions: Therapists create a safe space where each family member can voice their experiences and feelings without fear of judgment or retaliation. These sessions use interactive exercises to rebuild empathy and understanding among family members.

- Behavioral Analysis: Therapists work with the family to identify and analyze patterns of narcissistic behavior and their impact on family dynamics. This insight helps develop strategies to mitigate negative interactions and promote positive ones.

- Empowerment Strategies: Families are given practical tools to set boundaries, communicate effectively, and protect their emotional well-being. This empowerment is crucial in breaking the cycle of manipulation and control often seen in narcissistic relationships.

Mindfulness-Based Stress Reduction (MBSR)

The psychological toll of co-parenting with a narcissist cannot be understated. Mindfulness-Based Stress Reduction offers a therapeutic countermeasure, teaching individuals how to anchor themselves in the present moment, thus reducing anxiety and stress. MBSR incorporates techniques such as:

- Guided Meditation: Participants are guided through meditation practices focusing on breath and body awareness, helping to center thoughts and emotions.

- Mindful Movement: Gentle yoga and other mindful movements are introduced, encouraging a deeper connection between mind and body, fostering relaxation and stress relief.

- Daily Mindfulness Practices: Individuals are encouraged to incorporate mindfulness into their daily routines, transforming mundane activities into moments of mindfulness, thereby reducing overall stress levels.

Art and Creative Therapies

For children especially, articulating feelings about their narcissistic parent can be daunting. Art and creative therapies offer a non-verbal outlet for expressing complex emotions. Children (and adults) can explore and communicate their feelings through painting, drawing, music, and drama in a supportive environment. These therapies:

- Enhance Emotional Expression: Creative outlets provide a safe medium for expressing feelings that might be difficult to articulate verbally.

- Build Self-Esteem: Engaging in creative activities can boost confidence, providing a sense of accomplishment and self-worth.

- Facilitate Healing: The act of creation can be therapeutic in itself, helping to process and heal from emotional trauma.

Integrative Body-Mind Training

This cutting-edge therapeutic practice focuses on the interconnectedness of the body and mind. Integrative Body-Mind Training (IBMT) combines meditation, breathing exercises, and mindfulness to improve emotional regulation and resilience. Its application in the context of coping with a narcissistic co-parent includes:

- Enhanced Awareness: IBMT helps individuals become more aware of their emotional triggers and physical sensations, allowing for better management of responses. This is very helpful because knowing what triggers you empowers you and will ultimately make using the Grey Rock Method easier.

- Stress Reduction: Regular practice of IBMT has been shown to reduce stress and anxiety levels, providing a sense of calm in the face of co-parenting challenges.

- Emotional Regulation: By fostering a deeper connection between body and mind, individuals learn to regulate their emotions more effectively, reducing the likelihood of reactive behaviors that feed and encourage the narcissist.

In the shadow of narcissism, this therapeutic approach helps restore you and gives you the strength needed to be a stable co-parent. Dynamic family therapy rebuilds disrupted bonds, MBSR offers solace in mindfulness, narrative therapy reclaims personal stories, and art and creative therapies unlock emotional expression. Integrative Body-Mind

Training fortifies the connection between body and mind, equipping families with the resilience to navigate the complexities of co-parenting with a narcissist. Through these innovative practices, hope is renewed, and families are put on a path toward a future where emotional well-being is not just a possibility but a reality.

COMMUNITY LED INITIATIVES FOR CO-PARENTING SUPPORT

Support groups for survivors of narcissistic abuse allow you to hear stories from others who are also co-parenting with narcissistic ex-partners and serve as a potent reminder: you are not alone. These narratives validate personal experiences and offer diverse perspectives on coping strategies that might not have been considered previously. In this environment, experiences and lessons are shared, not just about surviving but also raising emotionally secure children.

Mentorship Programs

The journey of co-parenting with a narcissistic ex-partner is a path well-trodden by many. Support groups often establish mentorship programs, pairing individuals newly navigating these challenges with those who have found a way to manage effectively. This one-on-one support system provides practical advice and emotional backing, creating a lifeline during particularly challenging times.

Creating Safe Spaces

Perhaps the most critical role these community initiatives play is in creating safe spaces for individuals to express their fears, frustrations, and hopes. Within these circles, co-parents find acceptance and encouragement to speak openly without judgment. Shared strategies on how to deal with a narcissistic ex can be helpful and supportive. These spaces, whether physical meeting rooms or virtual chat rooms, become sanctuaries where healing begins and resilience is built.

PREDICTING FUTURE TRENDS IN CO-PARENTING PRACTICES

One emerging trend is the rise of AI-driven solutions designed to mitigate the complexities of co-parenting. Imagine applications not just scheduling appointments but predicting potential conflicts and suggesting resolutions based on past interactions. These AI algorithms could analyze communication patterns to warn parents when discussions are veering into potentially harmful territory, encouraging a pause or shift in tone to maintain constructive dialogues.

Another area ripe for innovation is virtual reality (VR) and its application in co-parenting scenarios. VR could offer a unique medium for children to spend time with each parent, regardless of physical distance. Through immersive experiences, a child could read a book, play a game, or explore a virtual world with the non-custodial parent, enriching their relationship and maintaining a strong bond.

Furthermore, integrating blockchain technology in co-parenting agreements could revolutionize tracking commitments and resolving disputes. By creating immutable records of agreements, payments, and schedules, blockchain offers a transparent and unalterable history of co-parenting interactions. This technology could drastically reduce conflicts over what was agreed upon, as every transaction and interaction would be securely logged and easily verifiable.

As we look to the future, these trends offer a glimpse into the potential transformations in co-parenting practices. From AI and VR to blockchain technology, the landscape of co-parenting is set to evolve in ways that prioritize healthy family dynamics, clear communication, and, most importantly, the well-being of children. These innovations and practices promise to simplify the logistics of co-parenting and make it significantly easier to co-parent or parallel parent with a narcissistic ex successfully.

Conclusion

We have looked at the complex terrain of understanding narcissism and its profound impacts on co-parenting dynamics. Through the chapters, we have unfolded practical strategies for either co-parenting or parallel parenting with a narcissistic ex-partner. This journey has been one of empowerment, resilience, and hope, giving you strength and insight.

Highlighting the book's main points, we began by recognizing the hallmarks of narcissistic behaviors and their disruptive influence on parenting arrangements. We delved into the critical decision between co-parenting and parallel parenting, laying out the groundwork for making an informed choice suitable to your unique situation. The significance of setting firm boundaries, navigating legal and financial challenges, and fostering personal growth post-divorce has been underscored. We discussed the importance of adapting these strategies to cater to diverse family dynamics and the potential of embracing innovative practices in co-parenting.

The key takeaways stress that while navigating co-parenting with a narcissist presents undeniable challenges, it also carves out an opportunity for profound personal growth, fortified parent-child relationships, and a nuanced understanding of healthy boundaries and communication. It will not be easy, and you will face many obstacles, but you can persevere and flourish.

Please apply the strategies discussed in this book to your co-parenting situations. Seek support from professionals and peers when necessary, use co-parenting apps, and always prioritize your well-being and your children's. There is no easy fix; steady yourself, commit to your children, use the Grey Rock Technique, and do not empower the narcissist by reacting.

Thank You

I hope you have enjoyed this book. I would love to hear your thoughts on this book.

Many readers are unaware of how difficult it is to get reviews and how much they help authors like me.

I would greatly appreciate it if you could support me and help get the word out to others about this book.

To leave a review, please either click on/ or use the link below or scan the QR code with your phone. I am very grateful for your support.

https://www.amazon.com/review/create-review/?ie=UTF8&channel=glance-detail&asin=B0CWCTNJB6

REFERENCES

- https://my.clevelandclinic.org/health/diseases/9742-narcissistic-personality-disorder*Narcissistic Personality Disorder: Symptoms & Treatment*

- https://www.psychologytoday.com/us/blog/the-legacy-of-distorted-love/201802/how-narcissistic-parenting-can-affect-children*How Narcissistic Parenting Can Affect Children*

- https://www.mindtools.com/axtfdfb/dealing-with-manipulative-people*Dealing With Manipulative People - Standing Your Ground*

- https://www.choosingtherapy.com/narcissistic-supply/ *What Is Narcissistic Supply?*

- https://www.psychologytoday.com/us/blog/the-legacy-of-distorted-love/201802/how-narcissistic-parenting-can-affect-children*How Narcissistic Parenting Can Affect Children*

- https://www.apa.org/topics/resilience/guide-parents-teachers*Resilience guide for parents and teachers*

- https://motherhoodandmayhem.online/explain-narcissism-to-child/*6 Tips for Explaining Narcissism to a Child*

- https://www.verywellmind.com/the-grey-rock-method-7483417*Can the Grey Rock Method Protect You From Toxic Behavior?*

- https://grace-being.com/love-relationships/setting-boundaries-with-a-narcissist/*Setting Boundaries with a Narcissist - 16 Tips & Examples*

- https://www.thebump.com/a/co-parenting-apps *The Best Co-Parenting Apps of 2024*

- https://talkingparents.com/parenting-resources/coparent-manipulating-your-child *What to Do When a Co-Parent is Manipulating Your Child*

- https://www.custodyxchange.com/topics/divorce/divorce-narcissist.php *Divorcing a Narcissist & Getting Child Custody From Them*

- https://www.forbes.com/sites/jefflanders/2012/12/11/financial-strategies-for-divorcing-a-narcissist/ *Financial Strategies for Divorcing A Narcissist*

- https://oplaw.com/blog/2023/may/creating-a-parenting-plan-with-a-narcissist/ *Creating a Parenting Plan with a Narcissist*

- https://www.micklinlawgroup.com/8-guidelines-guard-yourself-from-narcissist-divorce/ *8 Guidelines to Guard Yourself from a Narcissist in Divorce -*

- https://freedmarcroft.com/parallel-parenting-an-alternative-approach-for-high-conflict-co-parents/ *Parallel Parenting: An Alternative Approach for High-Conflict Co-Parents*

- https://www.verywellfamily.com/what-is-a-parallel-parenting-plan-and-how-to-make-one-5208661 *What Is a Parallel Parenting Plan? And How to Make One*

- https://www.awfamilylaw.com/blog/2023/july/how-to-co-parent-with-a-narcissistic-ex/ *How to Co-Parent with a Narcissistic Ex*

- https://theriveter.co/voice/parallel-parenting-changes-what-we-thought-we-knew-about-divorce/ *Parallel Parenting Changes What We Thought We Knew About Divorce*

- https://www.choosingtherapy.com/setting-boundaries-with-a-narcissist/ *15 Tips for Setting Boundaries With a Narcissist*

- https://www.lawinfo.com/resources/child-custody-lawyers/enforcing-a-custody-order.html *Enforcing a Custody Order*

- https://www.weinbergerlawgroup.com/blog/newjersey-child-parenting-issues

/parenting-with-a-high-conflict-ex-10-strategies-for-success/*Parenting With A High-Conflict Ex: 10 Strategies For Success*

- https://www.psychologytoday.com/us/blog/living-on-automatic/202301/hel ping-children-cope-with-a-narcissistic-parent*Helping Children Cope With a Narcissistic Parent*

- https://www.ourfamilywizard.com/blog/creating-perfect-parenting-plan-6-ste ps*Creating a Perfect Parenting Plan in 6 Steps*

- https://www.ecmediation.com/four-strategies-for-mediating-a-high-conflict-d ivorce/*Four Strategies for Mediating a High Conflict Divorce*

- https://www.child-encyclopedia.com/divorce-and-separation/according-exper ts/parenting-plans-following-separationdivorce-developmental*Divorce and separation: Parenting plans*

- https://www.healthline.com/health/parenting/co-parenting-with-a-narcissist *Co-Parenting with a Narcissist: Tips for Making It Work*

- https://www.itsovereasy.com/insights/how-to-turn-your-divorce-into-an-opp ortunity-for-personal-growth*How to Turn Your Divorce into an Opportunity for Personal Growth*

- https://www.collinsfamilylaw.com/blog/2024/february/creating-a-positive-co -parenting-relationship-af/*Creating a Positive Co-Parenting Relationship After Divorce*

- https://www.helpguide.org/articles/parenting-family/step-parenting-blended-f amilies.htm*Blended Family and Step-Parenting Tips*

- https://farzadlaw.com/divorcing-a-narcissist/how-protect-child-narcissistic-fat her-mother*How to Protect Your Child From a Narcissistic Parent*

- https://www.healthline.com/health/parenting/co-parenting-with-a-narcissist *Co-Parenting with a Narcissist: Tips for Making It Work*

- https://www.goldenparent.com/golden-parent-blog/multicultural-family-pare nting*Multicultural Families: Navigating Challenges of Parents and ...*

- https://greatergood.berkeley.edu/article/item/what_multicultural_families_c an_teach_kids_about_character *What Multicultural Families Can Teach Kids About Character*

- https://psychcentral.com/disorders/how-to-talk-to-someone-with-narcissistic -tendencies *10 Ways to Talk to Someone with Narcissistic Tendencies*

- https://www.medicalnewstoday.com/articles/co-parenting-with-a-narcissist#:~ :text=Set%20boundaries&text=discussing%20anything%20regarding%20child %20care,personal%20against%20them%20in%20future *5 tips for co-parenting with a narcissist - Medical News Today*

- https://www.psychologytoday.com/us/blog/the-legacy-of-distorted-love/201 802/how-narcissistic-parenting-can-affect-children *How Narcissistic Parenting Can Affect Children*

- https://www.verywellfamily.com/what-is-a-parallel-parenting-plan-and-how-t o-make-one-5208661 *What Is a Parallel Parenting Plan? And How to Make One*

- https://www.parentingforbrain.com/covert-narcissist-mother/ *9 Signs of a Covert Narcissistic Mother - Parenting For Brain*

- https://talkingparents.com/blog/combating-harassment-from-co-parent *Combating Harassment from Your Co-Parent | TalkingParents*

- https://www.pacer.org/webinars/cmh/Crisis-Management-Plan.pdf *Crisis Management Plan: Support for Children and Youth ...*

- https://www.thebump.com/a/co-parenting-apps *The Best Co-Parenting Apps of 2024*

- https://www.canadianlawyermag.com/practice-areas/family/technology-could -be-a-game-changer-in-settling-family-law-disputes-innovation-forum-attende es-hear/375250 *Technology could be a game-changer in settling family law ...*

- https://www.psychologytoday.com/us/blog/the-legacy-distorted-love/202203 /should-you-take-your-narcissistic-parent-family-therapy *Should You Take Your Narcissistic Parent to Family Therapy?*

- https://www.verywellmind.com/how-to-find-a-narcissistic-abuse-support-group-5271477*How to Find a Narcissistic Abuse Support Group*

-

Made in the USA
Las Vegas, NV
08 December 2024

13566776R00085